Gospel of the Trinity

Exploring the Gospel of John

— PATRICK WHITWORTH —

Sacristy
Press

Sacristy Press
PO Box 612, Durham, DH1 9HT

www.sacristy.co.uk

First published in 2023 by Sacristy Press, Durham

Sacristy Limited, registered in England & Wales, number 7565667

British Library Cataloguing-in-Publication Data
A catalogue record for the book is available from the British Library

ISBN 978-1-78959-282-5

For Rachel, Louisa, Sophia, David, and their families

Contents

Foreword

Nearly ten years after bringing us the first of his explorations of the New Testament Gospels, Patrick Whitworth now brings the series to a conclusion with this wonderful walk through John's account of the life, death and resurrection of Jesus. The Gospel author, who often refers to himself as "the one who Jesus loved", has produced a work that is similarly much beloved and which has held a special place in the hearts of Bible readers through the centuries thanks to its sense of intimacy, joyful exultation of a new life to be lived and its unique approach compared to the preceding synoptic Gospels.

Patrick is not only a prolific writer but an enthusiastic and fearless traveller. The success and enjoyment of any tour is made by the skill of the guide, and like the very best expedition leader, Patrick leads this journey through John drawing attention to the main "sites", revealing hidden gems along the way and setting the events in historical context as well as modern-day relevance.

Many years of preaching, teaching and pastoring church communities and study-groups are evident as Patrick delves into the text. Going beyond pure exegesis, the pages of this book are peppered with anecdotes, amusing stories and challenging applications to make the message clear and relevant. Being able to see the big picture is a gift, and as our attention is drawn to overarching themes that run through, not only this Gospel but the whole of Scripture, we find individual incidents held together and somehow given greater significance.

In this examination of the text, we start with the extraordinary overture of the prologue before discovering the seven signs and seven discourses, which reveal so much of the unique character, power and purpose of Jesus. He is a life-giver, but beyond that we clearly see the way in which each member of the Trinity, Father, Son and Spirit, are inextricably connected. As Patrick neatly expresses it, we find, "The

Gospel of the sending Father, the Incarnate Son and the life-giving Spirit. What becomes clear is that to know one is to know all" (p. 96).

The focus of the second half of the book is the events and the interactions surrounding the death and resurrection of Jesus. We are treated to a fascinating comparison of how the different Gospel writers reveal in their accounts the key themes that are unique to them. John, of course, highlights the life-giving sacrifice of Jesus for each who will believe and trust in him, but Patrick also shares the lovely reflection that a new family, a new community is formed at the foot of the cross.

Gospel of the Trinity makes an enriching read for anyone hungry for a deeper knowledge and understanding of this beautiful Gospel. It is worth taking time to read slowly and ponder the words of truth and grace. This book would also be a great companion for homegroups who want to make the journey together and the questions that can be found towards the back will stimulate thought and discussion.

The foreword of the first book in this series, focusing on the Gospel of Luke and the book of Acts, was written in 2014 by Alison Morgan who ascertained, "The twenty-first century is proving to be an interesting time. Likened by one commentator to being cast adrift in tossing seas on a raft with no map" (p. iv). Little could we have known quite how "interesting" the next few years were to become. Reeling from a global pandemic, devastated by the agony of war, suffering from a cost-of-living crisis and deeply worried about the environmental condition of our planet, the question remains and has intensified, "how best to live in this uncertain place" (p. iv)? The Gospel of John draws us back to Jesus and his offer of life for all who will believe and put their faith in him. As we turn the pages, we find an invitation to "come and see", to believe and to receive, to find nourishment and liberation, grace and truth, love and community.

John was to leave his home in Jerusalem and end his days on the island of Patmos. I write this foreword in my new island home in Guernsey, in the Channel Islands. I recently discovered the wonderful Guilles-Alles library in St Peter Port. When the library first opened, a window above the door was inscribed, "INGREDERE UT PROFICIAS", which translates, "enter so you may profit". I am delighted to commend this book to you and pray that as you enter its pages and allow Patrick to lead you through, you would richly profit.

"The great call to all humanity issued by Jesus is to believe in the Son of God and through him to faith in the Father who sent him. In this way, people come into the light, enjoy life, pass from condemnation to life, and experience grace and love." (p. 84)

Amen to that!

Sarah Couchman
2023

Preface

We might be hard pushed to decide which of these periods of English literature was the most significant: the late sixteenth century which included the Prayer Book, the Authorised Version of the Bible of 1611 and the plays of Shakespeare; the Romantic Poets of the late eighteenth century, including Keats and Wordsworth, or the nineteenth century novelists, including Jane Austen, Charles Dickens, the Brontës and George Eliot, among others. Many I suspect would choose the first period. But in terms of world literature, the period from c.AD 60 to AD 95, a mere 30 years or so, which produced the Gospels of Mark, Matthew, Luke and John (their possible chronological order) must be the most significant time of all. Unlike the Qur'an, which might spring to the mind of some as a contender, the story of Jesus was not given as a piece of dictation in a specific language (Arabic) to a single individual (Mohammad) in a series of visions, but rather, as the Apostle Peter says, different and varied men were moved by the Spirit and spoke from God (2 Peter 1:21). In fact, it is this extraordinary combination of human personality and divine inspiration (the Holy Spirit) which makes the Gospels so compelling, reflecting likewise the similar combination of the divine and human which made Jesus the Man who was and is God.

Four quite different individuals were chosen and inspired to write down the story of Jesus for all time. They have been well characterized by Robin Griffith-Jones as the Rebel (Mark) the Rabbi (Matthew), The Chronicler (Luke) and the Mystic (John). The first Evangelist was Mark, a man in a hurry, probably writing in Rome during the first period of sustained persecution of the Church and recording the memories of Peter, the leading Apostle, in the great and overbearing imperial city. The second was Matthew, one of the Apostles, writing from memory and from sources, including Mark and others, who wanted both to equip the Judean church and demonstrate that Jesus fulfilled all Jewish expectations of the Messiah. The third Evangelist was Luke, a Gentile, a companion of the Apostle Paul, a Doctor of the body and soul, a gifted historian of Jesus and the Early Church (The Acts), who by ethnicity and inclination had a heart, like Jesus, for the outsider and the marginalized. And lastly John, the Beloved Disciple, the reflective-one who for 50 years had waited to put pen to parchment or papyrus and record the story of the Word made Flesh in a different way: full of symbols, fresh ideas, Jewish traditions and immeasurable theological language. These men, indeed moved by the Spirit, wrote from God himself.

Off and on over the last ten years, I have written these explorations of the Gospels, interspersed with other books on church history, ancient and modern. My own studies of the Gospels seek to show the unique aspect of each Gospel in the conviction that not only were the Gospels written as the Spirit guided the personalities of their authors, but also the same Spirit speaks *today* to every reader who genuinely and prayerfully seeks Jesus in these pages. Indeed, sometimes just a few verses torn from the Gospels by people, even violently opposed to Christianity, have led to their conversion (see *Forgive me Natasha* by Sergei Korudakov, Marshall Pickering, 1975). Of course, it has been a privilege and blessing to reflect on the Gospels. And these studies are just another part of that great stream of scholarship, exegesis and more devotional works that have come down the ages to the church and world on the Gospels themselves.

For reasons I later explain, I have called John's Gospel *The Gospel of the Trinity*: for more than any other Gospel John shows the inner relationship of Father, Son and Spirit in the story of human salvation. John's Gospel is *the handbook to the Trinity*, and as such is fathomless, profound and luminous. John loves symbols as Jesus himself loved explaining spiritual truth in symbolic language. John uses allegories rather than parables, signs rather than miracles, interactive conversations rather than sermons, to explain the meaning of the Word becoming Flesh. I hope this study will be a blessing to you, and open new vistas and possibilities.

Thank you to Sacristy Press for once again publishing another of my books: Dr Natalie Watson, my Editor, and the supporting team. Thank you to Benedict Books for their support. Thank you to Sarah Couchman, who served with me on the staff-team at Weston All Saints Bath for 20 years as a Lay Reader and now lives in Guernsey, for generously writing the Foreword. And thank you to my family and friends for their interest and support in writing this book, and of the series as a whole.

Patrick Whitworth
St Patrick's Day 2023

Introduction

This is the last in a series of explorations in which I seek to pick out the unique theme of each Gospel. The Gospel of Matthew I characterized as *The Gospel of Fulfilment.* This book was placed first in the New Testament by the compilers for precisely that reason: i.e., that Matthew was at pains to show Jesus truly was the Messiah, and that he fulfilled in his life the many prophecies of the Old Testament. It is also a Gospel that gave the disciples a *vade mecum* (a guide) to discipleship, for it recalls much of Jesus's teaching about the lived Christian life, as in the Sermon on the Mount.

The Gospel of Mark I introduced as *The Gospel of the Kingdom*, since through this breathless depiction of Jesus's life and ministry, Mark is determined to demonstrate that the Kingdom of God is different from all known human kingdoms or empires, and that Jesus as the King was and is quite unlike any other human ruler.

The Gospel of Luke I described as *The Gospel of the Outsider*, for much of its material is focused on people likely to be overlooked, whether it is women like Mary, the Mother of Jesus, whose birth narratives he uniquely records; shepherds in the fields at Bethlehem; the Samaritan who is the hero of the parable that bears that name; the Gentiles, of whom Luke was most probably one; or the dying thief.

Now we come to the last of the four Gospels, which I have characterized *The Gospel of the Trinity.* I hope I can make it clear in the course of this book that there are good grounds for giving John's Gospel this title. Perhaps only Luke comes close to displaying the role of each member of the Trinity as vividly as John, only he does so in a different way. Luke shows the role of the Spirit in the incarnation, especially in the birth narratives recalling the annunciation (see Luke 1:26–38,39–45), and in the mission of Jesus (Luke 10:21). And following on from his Gospel, in the Acts of the Apostles, Luke pre-eminently shows us the role of the Spirit in the mission of the Church in its early years. However, John shows us the mysterious inner workings of the Trinity and the relationship of each with the others and together. No Gospel has a more exalted description of Jesus and his status: John describes Jesus as the Word made flesh, pre-existent before his incarnation as the eternal Son of the Father, dwelling by his side, and the bringer of all life, light and grace. Furthermore, Jesus continually recalls his relationship with his Father and their respective roles in salvation. In John 17, we eavesdrop on the longest prayer between Jesus and the Father. It concerns the future mission of the Church and the relationship of Father, Son and disciple. In John's Gospel, Jesus teaches more about the activity of the Spirit in the Upper Room discourses and his future role in the believer as Comforter, Advocate and Paraclete than in any other Gospel (John 14–16). John also records Jesus telling Nicodemus that it is the same Spirit who brings about a second birth (John 3:5–8). Towards the very end of the Gospel, Jesus breathes the Spirit over his disciples in prophetic anticipation of Pentecost (John 20:22).

These descriptions show us the inner dynamic and the place of the Trinitarian Godhead at the centre of the story. And consequent upon that, men and women are called to believe in the one they can touch, see, watch and hear, namely the Word made flesh, and by believing have eternal life (John 20:31).

Before plunging into the narrative of this extraordinary Gospel, we must ask a few basic questions: who was John, the author? When and where did he write? And what is the structure of the Gospel and its overriding message and theology? Before taking the plunge, we will consider these questions in turn.

Who was the author of the fourth Gospel?

There are several views among scholars as to the identity of John the Evangelist, or the author of the fourth Gospel. One view is that the Gospel was written by John the Elder, who reportedly lived in Ephesus at the same time as the Apostle John (who went to live there, quite possibly before the destruction of Jerusalem in AD 70). In this theory, John the

Elder is considered to be the anonymous Beloved Disciple, repeatedly mentioned in the Gospel.[1] It is a view that has gained traction in recent years both in Britain and on the Continent.

The Beloved Disciple is mentioned a number of times in the Gospel. In John 13, he is described as the one reclining next to Jesus at the Last Supper (John 13:23). He is also described as standing close to Mary, the Mother of Jesus, at the crucifixion (John 19:26). He is the one who bears witness to the death of Jesus on the cross and gives testimony to the separation of blood and serum when a spear is thrust into Jesus's side (John 19:34,35). He is also one of the two disciples who run to the tomb with Peter on the morning of the resurrection (John 20:2ff.). Furthermore, proponents of this theory believe that he is present at other occasions in the Gospel: as one of the two unnamed disciples at Jesus's baptism (although one of these is later named as Andrew (John 1:40)) and at the great catch of fish in John 21 (see 1:37 and 21:2b). Finally, the Beloved Disciple is mentioned twice after the great catch of fish in the subsequent conversation between Peter and Jesus on the beach in Galilee in the Gospel epilogue (21:7,20). The issue then is whether the author or Evangelist of the fourth Gospel is the Beloved Disciple, identified by many as John the Elder, and known to the early Church as living in Ephesus, *or* whether the Beloved Disciple is the Apostle John, the son of Zebedee, who is also the author of the fourth Gospel. There are two lines of enquiry that can help us to answer this question: the *first* is the internal evidence of the Gospel, informed by the narrative and information from the other Gospels, especially Mark (which is based on Peter's reminiscences), and the *second* is evidence from the authors of the first four centuries of the Church.

Although some scholars find it difficult to identify the Beloved Disciple with the Apostle John who is author of the fourth Gospel, it would seem the most natural explanation. It must surely be unlikely that the place of greatest proximity and indeed intimacy with Jesus at the Last Supper would have been given to someone *other than one of the Apostles*. We

---

[1] Richard Bauckham, *The Testimony of the Beloved Disciple* (Grand Rapids, MI: Baker Academic, 2009), pp. 73ff. This follows the views of Martin Hengel in *The Johannine Question*, trans J. Bowden (London: SCM Press, 1989).

are expressly told that the one Jesus loved was by implication one of the Twelve, or as the text says, "one of them" (i.e., the Apostles) was reclining next to Jesus at the Last Supper (see John 13:23). The Last Supper was a meal for Jesus and his 12 Apostles, including Judas. Indeed, in Mark's Gospel, which is based on Peter's account of the event, which was given to Mark in Rome (1 Peter 5:13), we are told categorically that "when evening came, Jesus arrived with the Twelve (*dōdeka*). While they were reclining at the table eating, he said, 'I tell you the truth one of you will betray me—one who is eating with me'" (Mark 14:17,18). Furthermore, it is unlikely that *anyone other than an Apostle* would have been told the news of the empty tomb by Mary Magdalene on the first Easter morning. Equally, it would be unlikely that another John would have been present on the beach in Galilee, especially when we have been told earlier that the two sons of Zebedee were present in the boat (John 21:2), and that it was the one designated as the Beloved Disciple (rather than Peter) who recognized the stranger on the shore telling them to cast their nets on the right side of the boat (John 21:7). The supposition must be that the Beloved Disciple was one of the Twelve, and since there is some self-disclosure that the Beloved Disciple (John 13:23) is also the author of the Gospel (John 21:24), the most natural deduction must be that the Beloved Disciple is John the Apostle.

This seems the most natural explanation from the internal evidence of John and Mark's Gospels taken together, and it appears to be corroborated by the most straightforward reading of the early Church writers, some of whom are called the Church Fathers. There appears to be five of these writers who have a bearing on this matter: Papias, Irenaeus, Eusebius, Clement of Alexandria and Jerome. In addition, Polycrates has an interesting piece on John which we shall consider.

Papias was the Bishop of Hierapolis (*c.*AD 60–130), which was near Laodicea and a place known for its hot springs. Although most of his extensive works (e.g., the five volumes of the *Sayings of Our Lord*) are lost, Papias is quoted by both Irenaeus and Eusebius. Eusebius recalls how he sought to learn from any presbyter who had known any of these

Apostles: Andrew, Peter, Philip, Thomas, James, John and Matthew.[2] We have to imagine priests or presbyters coming to Hierapolis and telling Papias what they knew of the Apostles and their work. Furthermore, Eusebius goes on to recall that Papias distinguished between John the Evangelist and John the Elder, both of whom were buried at Ephesus, and he states that it was John the Elder who was exiled and wrote the book of Revelation.[3] Not only was Papias's work recorded by Eusebius in his *History* written in the fourth century, but scholars believe that Papias was one of the sources of the first known list of New Testament books of the Bible, called the Muratorian Canon. And, in an interesting introduction to the listing of the fourth Gospel by the author of the so-called Muratorian Canon, Eusebius writes:

> The fourth of the Gospels is of John, one of the disciples. To his fellow-disciples and bishops, who were encouraging him, he said: "fast with me today for three days, and whatever will be revealed to each of us, let us tell one another". The same night it was revealed to Andrew, one of the apostles, that all should certify what John wrote in his own name.[4]

If Papias gives us some evidence, including the fragment called the Muratorian Canon, as to the writing and attribution of the fourth Gospel, later used by others, he is not the only one. Others who follow him are Irenaeus, the Bishop of Lyons (c.AD 130–202), Clement of Alexandria (the theological teacher and apologist) and Jerome (c.347–420).

Irenaeus refers to John's Gospel frequently in his great work against the Gnostics called *Against Heresies* (*Adversus haereses*). So, in Book III of this work, Irenaeus lists the authors of the Gospels, saying, "Afterwards, John the disciple of the Lord, who also leaned upon his breast [i.e., the

---

2   Eusebius, *History of the Church III:39* (Harmondsworth: Penguin Classics, 1989), p. 102.

3   Eusebius, *History of the Church III:39*, p. 102.

4   Cited by Bauckham, *Testimony of the Beloved Disciple*, p. 59, quoting Robert M. Grant, *Second Century Christianity: A Collection of Fragments* (London: SPCK, 1946), p. 118.

Beloved Disciple, John 13:23], did himself publish a Gospel during his residence at Ephesus in Asia."[5] Since Irenaeus was raised in Smyrna in Asia and, before becoming Bishop of Lyons, knew church leaders in the area from the mid second century onwards, he is a reliable witness. Not only this—and this will be important to us in considering the purpose and audience of the Gospel later—Irenaeus tells us that "John, the disciple of the Lord, preaches this faith, and seeks, by the proclamation of the Gospel, to remove that error which by Cerinthus [a Gnostic] had been disseminated among men, and long-time previously by those termed Nicolaitans [see Revelation 2:15 and the church at Pergamum], who are an offset of that knowledge [*gnosis*] falsely so called."[6]

Moreover, Clement of Alexandria is recorded by Eusebius as saying, "Last of all, aware that the physical facts had been recorded in the Gospels, encouraged by his pupils and irresistibly moved by the Spirit, John wrote a spiritual Gospel."[7] And lastly, in his survey of the Church Fathers' attribution of the fourth Gospel to John the Apostle and son of Zebedee, Jerome wrote in his account of illustrious early Christians:

> John, the apostle whom Jesus most loved, the son of Zebedee and brother of James the Apostle, whom Herod, after the Lord's passion beheaded, was the last one to write a Gospel, at the request of the bishops of Asia, against Cerinthus and other heretics and especially against the growing doctrine of the Ebionites, who asserted that Christ did not exist before Mary. For this reason, he was compelled also to announce his divine nativity.[8]

The impression one gets is of an Apostle reluctant to write but being pressed into setting down his memory of the ministry of Jesus in such a way as to rebut growing heretical tendencies in Asia, particularly those

---

5   Irenaeus, *Adversus haereses*, Book III:I.1, TANF, Vol. 1 (Grand Rapids, MI: Eerdmans, 1975), p. 414.

6   Irenaeus, *Ad. Her.*, Book III:XI.1, p. 426.

7   Eusebius, *History of the Church* (*Ecc. Hist.*) *VI:14*, p. 192.

8   Jerome, *Vir illustris 9*, cited by Bauckham, *Testimony of the Beloved Disciple*, p. 67.

which came to be associated with Gnosticism and Neo-Platonism in both the Hellenic and Jewish worlds. This point is further confirmed by Eusebius in his record of the Evangelists and their writings. Writing in the first half of the fourth century in *The History of the Church*, he notes:

> Thus, John in his Gospel narrative records what Christ did when the Baptist had not yet been thrown into gaol, while the other three evangelists describe what happened after the Baptist's consignment to prison. Once this is grasped, there no longer appears to be a discrepancy between the gospels, because John deals with the early stages of Christ's career and the others cover the last period of his story.[9]

That Eusebius is right in his estimation of the chronology of John's Gospel is very questionable, since the entire second half from Chapter 12 onwards is centred on the final week of Jesus's earthly life and ministry. It is more likely, as we shall see, that the Gospel was not written strictly chronologically, but theologically, following its various themes. What we can take from this quote and the preceding ones, however, is that the early Church believed that it was the Apostle John who wrote the Gospel, and from the internal evidence of the Gospel it is quite natural to identify the Beloved Disciple, who indicates he is the author of the Gospel (19:35), with John the Apostle.

One other unlikely theory of authorship arises from a letter written by Polycrates, Bishop of Ephesus in the last decade of the second century, who writes to Victor of Rome about the date of Easter. In this letter, he names John as a "priest who wore the sacerdotal plate and who was a martyr and teacher of the church". This description is cited by Eusebius in his *History of the Church*.[10] Although it is true that John appeared to know the High Priestly family (18:15ff.), it is highly unlikely that he himself was a priest, and is certainly not the John mentioned in Acts 4:6, as some

---

[9]   Eusebius, *Ecc. Hist.*, p. 87.

[10] Eusebius, *Ecc. Hist.* 5:24.2–7, cited also by Bauckham, *Testimony of the Beloved Disciple*, p. 37.

have suggested.[11] As noted, the internal evidence of the Gospel suggests that the Beloved Disciple was the son of Zebedee, a fisherman from Galilee. Having considered the authorship of the Gospel, it is now time to consider the time and place of writing, and its structure and purpose.

The time and place of writing

We have already noted that the Gospel was written in Ephesus, and once again this is confirmed by the Church historian, Eusebius, who quotes Irenaeus: "All the clergy who in Asia came into contact with John, the Lord's disciple, testify that John taught the truth to them: for he remained with them till Trajan's time [AD 98–117]."[12] Eusebius tells how, as an old man, the Apostle John was carried around Ephesus on a litter from which he appealed to passers-by to love one another. Other stories are told of John seeking out the lost and bringing them back to God.[13] John the Apostle and son of Zebedee, and John the Elder, were both buried in Ephesus, and indeed a tomb marked as John the Apostle's burial place remains in the now-destroyed basilica close to the classical site of Ephesus.

The Gospel was probably written late in the first century, and certainly after the publication of the Synoptic Gospels. Once again Eusebius maintains that

> the three gospels already written were in circulation and copies had come into John's hands. He welcomed them, we are told and confirmed their accuracy but remarked that the narrative only lacked the story of what Christ had done first of all at the beginning of his mission.[14]

---

[11]   Bauckham, *Testimony of the Beloved Disciple*, p. 48.

[12]   Eusebius, *Ecc. Hist.*, Bk III, 23, p. 83, citing Irenaeus, *AH* II.33.2.

[13]   Eusebius, *Ecc. Hist.*, Bk III, 23c, pp. 85–6.

[14]   Eusebius, *Ecc. Hist.*, Bk III, 23, p. 87.

As we have seen already, the latter remark is unconvincing, since John's Gospel adds little to the earliest part of the narrative of Jesus's ministry. In fact, if anything, apart from the Miracle in Cana of Galilee, John has less about the early ministry of Jesus. Nonetheless, the notion of John's being the last Gospel written, with the author having knowledge of the other three, is well attested, not only by Eusebius, but by Irenaeus and Clement of Alexandria as well. It is normally thought that Mark's Gospel was written first, and, being a record of the Apostle Peter's memories, is thought to have been written around the time of Peter's martyrdom in AD 64. Thereafter Matthew and Luke were written, using Mark as a source, a common source called Q (for the German word *Quelle*, meaning source), and independent sources unique to each of them. Scholars often date their writing to after the destruction of Jerusalem in AD 70. Matthew's Gospel emerges from the Judean church with a strong Jewish focus, and Luke's Gospel was quite possibly written in or around Antioch and Caesarea when Paul was standing trial in the latter city in *c.*AD 60 (see Acts 24–26), and therefore a little earlier. Luke's Gospel was most probably written by a Gentile who was also Paul's companion, and who addressed both the Gospel and Acts to one Theophilus, a Greek or Roman personage.

If John's Gospel was written and first published in Ephesus rather than Palestine or Rome, and as late as AD 90, it would reflect the following concerns of the Church: an anxiety over the growing influence of Gnosticism in the area; an awareness of the Jewish community in Ephesus and its relationship with the Church; and the growing influence of Neo-Platonism and Greek philosophy and thought. This resulted from the influence of Philo of Alexandria (*c.*25 BC–AD 50), who sought to straddle both Judaism and Greek philosophy in the East, and whose thinking would in time be further developed in the Neo-Platonism of Plotinus (*c.*AD 204–70). Although Jewish to the core, John would not be unaware of these influences, and they would in turn influence the writing of his Gospel and his Epistles. Moreover, he was increasingly aware of the opposition both of the synagogue and, more especially, of the Roman Empire. It was quite clear that emperor worship had reached new heights in the reigns of Nero (AD 54–68), Domitian (AD 81–96) and Trajan (AD 98–117). Christians who refused to sacrifice to the emperor were becoming targets of persecution and were being blamed or scapegoated for the mishaps of the empire, such as military defeat, flooding, earthquakes and famine.[15] Indeed, the late date of John's Gospel and its writing location of Ephesus influenced both the construction and content.

The construction and audience of the Gospel

As noted, it is most probable that John's was the last Gospel to be written, and that John knew the Synoptic Gospels of Mark, Luke and Matthew, which share common material. John set out to write a different Gospel, but with the same intent: to make Jesus known and to offer eternal life through belief or faith in him.[16] Here was the intent of the Gospel. It was evangelistic and aimed to bring life by inviting *belief* through telling the story of Jesus from before time and then through his incarnation, manifestation, mission and exaltation. There are a number of essential features of the Gospel.

It is divided into two overall sections (and this book also divides into two parts, which reflects that overall division). The first part (John 1–11) revolves around the *manifestation of the Word made flesh*, and the second part (John 12–21) revolves around the *exaltation of the Word and the mission of the Church*. The whole work is preceded by the Prologue (1:1–18) and concluded by the Epilogue (Chapter 21). These were not added later by the Ephesian church but were an integral part of the original Gospel.

The first part of the Gospel, which I am calling the "Manifestation of the Word made Flesh", is carefully constructed and runs up to and includes Chapter 11. In order to manifest the true nature of the Word made flesh, John constructs these first 11 chapters around a scheme. This begins with the Prologue, which is a kind of overture to the whole Gospel,

---

[15]   See Tertullian, *Apologia* xl, p. 47, Vol. III, TANF (New York: Cosimo, 2007).

[16]   See John 20:31: "But these are written that you may believe that Jesus is the Christ [Messiah, or Anointed One], the Son of God, and that *by believing*, you may have life in his name."

announcing its main themes and proceeding to show how Jesus enacts them in his incarnate life. There is an old adage that the Synoptic Gospels are history and John's Gospel theology, but it is a facile dichotomy. In fact, theology cannot be divorced from any of the Gospels, as I have sought to show in this series of Gospel explorations. And indeed, John's Gospel has as much in the way of historical detail as any. For instance, when it comes to recalling named places, John has 31, of which 17 are unique to his Gospel. Matthew names 35, but only eight are unique to him.[17] In other words, John is intent on locating stories about Jesus in historical places which may be verified. His work is both historical and theological, but it is devised around a strong theological theme of bringing new life to the Jewish nation and to the world.

It is in this context that John sets forth his scheme. He selects seven signs, which are miracles as well as demonstrations of the life-giving properties of the Word made flesh, and signs of Jesus's divinity. These seven signs begin with the Miracle at Cana and end with the Raising of Lazarus. Linked to these signs, sometimes loosely and sometimes more directly, are the seven sayings of Jesus, such as "I am the bread of Life" (John 6:48), "I am the Light of the World" (8:12), and "I am the resurrection and the life" (11:25). Interspersed between the seven signs—some of which are quite short, e.g., the Healing of the Nobleman's Son (John 4:43–54), while others, such as the Raising of Lazarus, occupy almost a whole chapter (11:1–44)—are seven dialogues and discourses. The dialogues give us some of the most illuminating conversations of the whole New Testament, such as the ones with Nicodemus (3:1–15), with the woman at the well (4:1–26), and with the sisters of Lazarus (11:17–37). Alongside these dialogues, John offers sometimes lengthy discourses in which Jesus teaches about his identity, his relationship with the Father, and later, in the Upper Room, about the coming of the Spirit. It is in these discourses that the Trinity is especially explored and the relationship of each member to the others in a way that is unique to John's Gospel.

Other facets of the Gospel which are distinctive are worth noting. Jerusalem is the main location for much of the action. There are only a

---

17 See Bauckham, *Testimony of the Beloved Disciple*, p. 98.

few times when Jesus moves outside Jerusalem in the narrative. These locations are Bethany beyond the Jordan (1:28), Cana of Galilee (2:1–11), Sychar in Samaria, and once again Cana (4:1–54), Galilee for the Feeding of the Five Thousand and the Walking on Water (6:1–71) and the escape from Jerusalem (10:40–42; 11:54). Almost all of the rest of the narrative is spent in Jerusalem with Jesus teaching and arguing with the Jews at the time of the Jewish feasts.

Another facet of John's writing is his love of symbolic language and allegory to explain the character of Jesus and his offer of life. This use of symbolic language, first used by Jesus himself, is evident throughout, and it gives the Gospel a resonance and depth of meaning which is unique. Finally, John himself freely makes editorial comments of great significance throughout. Indeed, the most famous verse in the Gospel, John 3:16, at the end of the conversation with Nicodemus, is one such editorial comment. Some think that there are between 109 and 165 such editorial additions in the Gospel, depending on one's reading of the text.[18]

If the first 11 chapters can be summarized as the "Manifestation of the Word made Flesh", the second part of the Gospel can be denoted the "Exaltation of the Word and the Mission of the Church". This second part of the Gospel, moving towards the Passion, begins in John 12, which is a kind of introduction to what will follow. Jesus is anointed by Mary for his burial (12:7). He then enters Jerusalem triumphantly (12:12–19). Some Greeks seek an interview, but Jesus is now naturally preoccupied with his coming death and passion, and they get no further than speaking to Philip (12:20–22). Jesus announces that the hour referred to in 2:4 has finally arrived: "The hour has come for the Son of Man to be glorified" (12:23,27). This glorification will happen through the crucifixion and resurrection, where Jesus will reveal the true extent of his love (13:1b). The Father confirms the identity and the destiny of the Son (12:28–33), while the Jewish leaders continue to protest and disbelieve him. Jesus's preferred phrase for his forthcoming death is being "lifted up" (12:32), which has within it the notion of exaltation as well as crucifixion. In other words, the crucifixion is to be an exaltation of all that Jesus is and stands for.

---

[18]   Bauckham, *Testimony of the Beloved Disciple*, p. 104.

The narrative proceeds swiftly from this bridge chapter. Jesus washes the disciples' feet at the Last Supper, which John makes the central action of this meal, highlighting the betrayal by Judas rather than the memorial of Jesus's death in bread and wine. Perhaps John thought he had intimated enough about this memorial feast in Chapter 6 (see 6:53–59) to need to say more about the institution of the Last Supper. The lengthy Upper Room discourse and the discourse outside the Temple (see 14:31c; Chapters 14–16) which follow are packed with teaching about the roles of the Father, Son and Holy Spirit and their relationship with each other and with the disciples. This is undoubtedly the most sustained teaching in the New Testament about the Trinity and their relationship with the disciples and future believers.

After Jesus's prayer for his disciples, often called his High Priestly Prayer (John 17), his arrest and trials—including a lengthy and revealing interview with Pilate (18:28–19:16)—Jesus is crucified. Emphasizing his Kingship and Kingdom, the crucifixion is shown as gathering a community around the cross (19:25–27), as well as completing the work of redemption Jesus came to achieve (19:30,34–35). The account of the resurrection demonstrates Jesus's bodily resurrection, but also his transformation to a new existence (see 20:17,20,27).

The Epilogue to the Gospel forms Chapter 21. In it, the great catch of fish is both a miracle and, as with so much else in the Gospel, a metaphor for the mission of the Church. This has been anticipated in the commissioning of the disciples in the resurrection appearance in the Upper Room, in which Jesus breathes the Spirit upon them and gives them authority to pronounce the forgiveness of sins (20:22,23). This action of Jesus is to be fulfilled on the day of Pentecost, but here it is anticipated. In preparation for his mission, Peter is restored and commissioned, and John himself is told he will live to a great age. All must follow Jesus, however (21:22b).

CHAPTER 1

Overture to the Gospel

The Prologue (John 1:1–18)

There are few more inspiring or inspired passages of Scripture than the first 18 verses of John's Gospel. Most of us know them as the last reading in the service of Lessons and Carols used at Christmas. The cadences and the words themselves often have a kind of mesmerizing effect, allowing us to revel in the language. But perhaps we do not always pause long enough to consider the meaning behind John's language. It is not called the Prologue for nothing, and I liken it to a kind of overture of the whole work. Overture comes from the French word *ouverture*, which literally means an opening before a work, whether a symphony or an opera. In an overture, some of the musical phrases appear which may be used later in the work. In the Prologue, John gives us some of the defining theological phrasing of his Gospel, and in particular the significance of the Word made flesh, or the incarnation. The key words and phrases that cascade through these verses are Word (*logos*), God (*theos*), life, light, darkness, testimony, witness, world, receive, believe, power, became flesh, grace, truth, glory, fullness, law, and made known. These words are the ones around which the Gospel is built, to which they remain seminal.

The creative word (1:1–5)

The title that John uses to introduce Jesus is the Word or the *logos*. *Logos* is the term used in the Septuagint (the Greek translation of the Old Testament made by 70 scholars in Alexandria) to translate the term "word" in the Old Testament Scriptures. It was used by the 70 Jewish scholars given the task of translation in the reign of Ptolemy III in the third century BCE. However, while it had Jewish origins, it was also familiar to the Greeks and in Hellenic thought generally. To the Jews or in the Hebrew Scriptures it meant the active word of God, which brought the world into existence from nothing. The *logos* was the "ruling fact of the universe",[19] the entity through whom reason and knowledge controls all the laws of the universe. This concept was also expressed by Philo (*c.*20 BC–AD 50), the Jewish Alexandrian philosopher. The Jewish definition stresses the creative fiat of Almighty God, while the Greek understanding highlights the rational organizing principle. Jesus as the *logos* is the one who, from eternity, can bring all things into existence as the Cosmic Son of God, and, as the Incarnate Lord and Christ, can bring into being the new resurrection community. It is a lot to encapsulate in a single word, and typical of John's evocative use of language guided by the Holy Spirit.

John goes on to say more about this Word, whom he later reveals as the Incarnate Christ. He says he was "in the beginning", indicating an eternal existence, meaning there was never a time that Jesus did not exist as the Word and also the Son, meaning in turn that there was never a time when the Father was not the Father. Both existed eternally as Father and Son, and if Arius, the fourth-century heretic, had chosen to believe this, rather than the Greek philosophy that suggested a single God, we would not have had the Arian controversy of the fourth century and the years of doctrinal struggle to establish the existence of the Trinity. This issue was hammered out initially in the Nicene Creed, in which Father and Son were said to be of a single substance (*homoousios*) but also individual beings. The phrase "in the beginning" reflects the opening words of the Bible and Genesis which declare, "In the beginning, God . . . " (Genesis 1:1). Thus, in the beginning was God and in the beginning was the Word or *Logos*. Neither existed without the other, Son and Father, and we shall come to the Spirit later in the Gospel.[20]

---

[19] William Temple, *Readings in St John's Gospel* (London: Macmillan, 1949), p. 4.

[20] For more on this see Patrick Whitworth, *Defining God: Athanasius and the Fourth-century Trinitarian Controversy* (Durham: Sacristy Press, 2023).

The next statement—which will be pivotal to the Gospel and begs the question about the identity of the Incarnate Jesus which runs throughout the Gospel, especially in the controversial dialogues with the Jews—is "and the Word was God". This would translate from the Greek original more literally as "God was the Word" (*kai theòs ēn o lógos*). In this statement lies the uniqueness of the Incarnate Word. This is the declaration of the Gospel about the identity of Jesus. It is behind the seven signs. It is behind the "I am" sayings, especially the one most inflammatory to the Jews: "before Abraham was, I am" (8:58), in which Jesus claims precedence over Abraham, the father of the nation (Genesis 12:1–4; 15:4–5) and entitlement to the divine name (Exodus 3:14). John further elaborates his meaning by saying not only was the Word God, but the Word was *with* God in the beginning.

In so saying, and at the outset of his Gospel, John strikes the opening chords of this overture. He presents a theme which will run throughout: in the controversies with Jews over his true identity and in answer to the demand of Philip to "show us the Father and that will be enough for us". Here Philip receives the unambiguous and reproving reply, "Don't you know me, Philip, even after I have been among you such a long time? Anyone who has seen me has seen the Father" (John 14:8–14). The theme recurs when, after the resurrection, in an expression of worship after seeing the risen Jesus's wounds, Thomas says, "My Lord and my God" (John 20:28).

Having composed the "chords" declaring the divinity of the Word, John now notates the creative power of the Word. Everything was made through him. This truth was expressed some years earlier, probably unknown to John, in Paul's letter to the Colossians, where the Apostle wrote, "For by him all things were created: things in heaven and on earth ... whether thrones or powers or rulers or authorities" (Colossians 1:16). For Paul, the Word was not only the agent of creation (through whom) but also the power behind creation (by whom). By the late fourth century, orthodox Christians came to believe that each member of the Trinity was engaged in the actions of the other. In other words, each had their role and being, but each shared in the actions of the other.

It is no wonder then, that since the Word is the creator of all that *is*, he is also the creator of that mysterious principle which we call life itself.

Life cannot yet be replicated (nor ever probably will be) by scientists of whatever kind. Yes, we can take the rudiments of life and reconstruct and redesign, but we cannot create from nothing. When it comes to that we are powerless. And when it comes to the highest organism in existence, the human brain with its trillions of connections, we still cannot account for consciousness, thought, personality or motivation. If the Word is quite simply the creator of life in the first place, however we describe it—in terms of the solar system in its immensity, the animal kingdom in its variety, or the planet Earth in its beauty—it must be no surprise that in his incarnate life Jesus remains the life force he always had been. Thus, John says, "in him was life and that life was the light of all people". Here is another vital "chord" to the overture. The incarnate Word will be a life-giver, and this note will be repeatedly struck in the Gospel: to the wedding party about to run out of wine, to Nicodemus stuck in his religious straitjacket, to the Samaritan woman needing water at midday, to the man born blind, and to Lazarus prematurely dead in his tomb. All needed life of a different kind. And the kind of life Jesus brings as the Incarnate Word is light-bearing. His life always enhances life and never destroys, diminishes or detracts.

But humans have a tendency to darkness. And we have plenty of examples to draw on, whether the wars of the twentieth century, the Holocaust, or now the unprovoked war with all its destruction and terror in Ukraine. It is human evil, darkness and the opposite of light-giving life. The Gospel will sound the chords of that darkness. It will be a continuous, insistent, escalating and rebarbative refrain. Indeed, in one of his edits after the conversation with Nicodemus, John says, "Light has come into the world, but people loved darkness instead of light because their deeds were evil" (3:19). But then the Apostle John, knowing first-hand the brutality of the Roman Empire from evidence in Asia in the late first century and the growing persecution of the Church, affirms "the light shines in the darkness, and the darkness has not overcome it". However strong the darkness, it will never extinguish the light (1:5).

The testimony of John the Baptist (1:6–8)

Witness or testimony is an important aspect of the thinking of this Gospel. Furthermore, the corroboration of evidence by a witness was firmly part of Jewish law and social interaction. Some have discerned that there are seven witnesses or types of witness in John's Gospel. Together they bear witness to the true identity of Jesus. The Word bears witness to himself in the conversation with Nicodemus. Thus, he says, "I tell you the truth, we speak of what we know and we testify to what we have seen, but still, you people do not accept our testimony" (3:11, see also 3:32). Later, principally in Chapter 8, when his identity is central to the discourse, Jesus on several occasions bears witness to himself (see 8:14,18). Moreover, Jesus's works and words are also brought forward as witnesses to his true identity (for works see 5:36; 10:25; 14:11; 15:24; and for words, 5:39ff.; 5:45ff.). Likewise, the Father bears witness to Jesus's true identity (see 5:31–36; 12:28b) and the Spirit also (see 15:26; 16:14). Again, we see in this Gospel the way in which the members of the Trinity mutually recognize and identify each other. The Trinity and the works and words of Jesus make five witnesses; two more remain.

Beyond them, the other main witnesses are John the Baptist, whose principal role in this Gospel is to identify Jesus as the Word made flesh or the Light of the World (1:7), and other people. We see the Baptist's witness and activity later in the chapter when identifying Jesus as the Lamb of God (1:29). Whereas in the Synoptic Gospels John is remembered for his ascetic lifestyle (eating locusts and wild honey), his excoriating preaching, his imprisonment and brutal death, here the author John simply presents the Baptist as a witness giving most valuable testimony. The final and seventh category of witness is human witness. There are people in John's Gospel who give a vivid human witness to the true identity of Jesus after their encounters with him. They include the woman at the well who said, "Come, see a man who told me everything I ever did. Could this be the Christ?" (4:29), and about whom John says in one of his editorial comments: "Many of the Samaritans from that town believed in him because of the woman's testimony, 'He told me everything I ever did'" (4:39). Then there is the man born blind (9:25), the crowd who witnessed the raising of Lazarus (12:17), and ultimately the disciples themselves (19:35; 21:24). Together, these seven witnesses, including the Trinity, give a powerful testimony of the identity of Jesus as the Lord and Christ. And of course seven is regarded as the perfect number in Judaism.Despite this, as John goes on to say in the Prologue, only some received him and found a new birth, while others of his own people rejected him.

The offer of new life (1:9–13)

Having begun the Prologue with breath-taking theological statements about the status and essence of the Word, and by emphasizing that the Word is the bringer of light and life to a world shrouded in moral and spiritual darkness, John moves into more narrowly defined territory. As we have seen, the Word has a unique human witness in John the Baptist, who was not the light himself but testified to the light who "was coming into the world". Nevertheless, although the world was made through the Word, in general it refused to recognize him while he was in it (1:10).

At this point, the Prologue moves to considering the human response to the coming of the Word. The key word John uses here is receive (*lambánō*), to which in this context he gives the meaning of believing "in his name" (1:12), which is therefore a kind of synonym for receiving the Word into our lives. Throughout the Gospel, such *receiving* means an acceptance based on belief, and it is a major chord in this opening overture. Furthermore, John describes this coming to believe as a process of new birth. The metaphor of birth has its root in Jesus's conversation with Nicodemus in John 3:3. This spiritual re-birth comes not through the normal means of physical birth, the desire of a parent, or from human will, but instead through the will of God (1:12,13). In this case, the seed of his Word generates new birth, and results in the elevation of a person *into a new sphere of living*, in which there is now an understanding resulting from knowing the Father, Son and Spirit, and which is an assumption of our lives (bodies, minds and spirits) into the life of the Father, Son and Spirit. This new sphere of life is described by the much-used phrase in John's Gospel of "eternal life".

Thus, at the end of the Gospel, John reminds his readers that he has written in order "that you may believe that Jesus is the Christ [Messiah], the Son of God, and that by believing you may have life in his name" (20:31). Furthermore, Jesus has given us a definition of eternal life in his great prayer of John 17, saying, "This is eternal life; that they may know you, the only true God, and Jesus Christ whom you have sent" (17:3). And of course, to know the Father through the Son requires the birth-giving power of the Spirit (see 3:6–8).

Having described the human response to the coming into the world of the Word, John adds some concluding verses to his Prologue about the incarnation, interspersed with a brief word of testimony concerning John the Baptist.

The grace and truth of the Word (1:14–18)

John re-iterates first of all the wonder of the Word taking on flesh in the incarnation. He simply tells us that "the Word became flesh and made his dwelling among us" (1:14). Matthew and Luke tell us how this happened in reality: how Mary conceived as a virgin, what Joseph thought, how each was addressed by an angel, telling them of God's purpose. If Matthew and Luke tell us the human/divine side of the story, John puts the incarnation in deeply theological terms: the Word became flesh, or as the hymn writer Charles Wesley put it in *Hark the Herald Angels sing*, "veiled in flesh the Godhead see". Writing some 300 years after John, Athanasius, Bishop of Alexandria, explained the incarnation in these daring terms: "For he became man that we might become divine: and he revealed himself through a body that we might receive an idea of the invisible Father; and he endured insults from men that we might inherit incorruption."[21] In other words, by the Word becoming enfleshed and becoming like us, only without sin, we in turn might become in him what we are not.

---

[21] Athanasius, *De Incarnatione* 54, ed. Robert W. Thomson (Oxford: Oxford University Press, 1971), p. 269.

After telling us that the Word took on flesh in the mystery of the incarnation and tabernacled (dwelt) among us, recalling the tabernacle among the Israelites (see Exodus 26), John goes on to give us some of the defining characteristics of the Incarnate Word and, in particular, his glory, another important Johannine word. Glory means the shining out of his inner nature. It is used throughout the Gospel, initially here and then in the first sign at Cana in Galilee, where we are told that Jesus revealed his glory in the first miracle or sign there (2:11), but more especially in connection with his passion and crucifixion (see 12:23ff.). It will be evident that it is in his sufferings and death that Jesus will especially reveal his glory and those two inner characteristics of his life: grace and truth. They could equally have been mercy or love and justice. The stamp of Jesus's life on earth was the combination of these two qualities, which are so often unable to live side by side in human affairs. He was full of grace and truth. Again and again, Jesus shows this combination with different people, from the woman at the well, to the woman caught in adultery; from the conversation with Pilate (19:8ff.), to the bystanders at the cross itself (19:25ff.). The point that John makes in the Prologue is that Jesus surpasses Moses, who brought only the Law, good though it was. Jesus brings truth in his teaching, but alongside this, free grace or unmerited love.

As his followers, we are to try through his Spirit to model grace and truth in our lives, not weakening the demands of the moral law or the way of life of the Beatitudes but enacting them through grace. As someone once said, we are to be G and T Christians. It is a difficult balance. The glory of Jesus was that he perfected the combination.

Finally, John ends his Prologue, which is so like an overture, with a great flourish, a crescendo of music with strings, wind and percussion. "No-one has ever seen God, but God the One and Only, who is at the Father's side has made him known" (1:18). Jesus is the perfect revelation of the Father. What we will be treated to in the coming chapters is that revelation in all its glory, in grace and truth, bringing light and life to Israel and to the world. Some will choose darkness, but others will come into his glorious light and find the life that endures eternally. The Prologue has more than whetted the appetite for what follows.

CHAPTER 2

Great Expectations

John 1:19–51

Before launching into the narrative of the Gospel, we must first recall
the nature of Israel and the Jerusalem of which John was so much a part
for many years, and about which he wrote so fully in his Gospel. For
although the construction of the Gospel is shaped as much theologically
as historically, it would be wrong to say that John in any way sacrificed
history or precise detail on the altar of theology. Instead, he married the
two in a unique way. If his childhood and school years (possibly taught
in the local synagogue in or near Capernaum) were spent in Galilee as
a son of Zebedee—a local well-to-do fisherman who had employees to
mend his nets (see Mark 1:19,20)—after the time spent with Jesus, his
later years were most probably in Jerusalem, before he moved to Ephesus.

There are two essential truths to know about Israel in *c*.AD 30. The
first is that it was occupied by the Romans. Following the conquest of
Jerusalem and Judea by the Roman General Pompey in 63 BC, the country
was annexed to Rome and increasingly governed from Antioch as part
of the eastern, Syrian province of the empire, although with a governor
and Roman soldiers billeted in Jerusalem. Herod the Great became a
client king of Judea, appointed by Caesar Augustus (Octavian, the great
nephew and heir of Julius Caesar), in 37 BC. He ruled until 4 BC, which
must have coincided with the birth of Jesus (see Matthew 2:1–12, where
the Magi come to Herod seeking to know the whereabouts of the infant
king, Jesus). Although Herod had sought to curry favour with the Jews
by rebuilding the Temple (John 2:20), he was nonetheless merciless in
using political power to shore up his dynasty and kill any incipient rival.

The *second* great truth about Israel at this time is the increasing expectation of the coming of the Messiah. The expectation of a Messiah, literally an anointed one, was translated into Greek with the word *Christos*, from which we get the title of Christ. The book of Daniel, itself forged during the experience of exile, expected a Son of Man or Messiah to inaugurate an apocalyptic age in which the Messiah would rule and peace would reign (see Daniel 7:1–14, Daniel 12 and Isaiah 11). The idea of a Jewish Messiah coming to deliver God's people from occupation and servitude grew during the era of the Second Temple (516 BC–AD 70). Indeed, for much of that time Judea and Jerusalem were under the control of the Seleucid Greeks, one of whom, Antiochus IV Epiphanes (ruled 175–164 BC), provoked the Jews into a rebellion led by Judas Maccabeus. This was a time in which Judaism sought to re-establish its own rule over its people and re-kindle the expectation of a Messiah (see 2 Maccabees 1:27–29, the Prayer of Jonathan).

In the period around AD 30 and the ministry of Jesus, the expectation of a coming Messiah was only increasing. Indeed, the Pharisaic movement or the *Hasīdīm*, a strongly pietistic and legalistic group, sought to use strict observance as a way of defining Judaism, thereby uniting the nation and weaponizing it against the Romans. The Pharisees were behind one such movement of first-century Israel. Others included the Scribes and the Sadducees. Still others, with a more monastic bent, were the Essenes and the Qumran community living in the Dead Sea area, responsible for painstakingly copying the Hebrew Scriptures and known for minute observance of the Law. Finally, there were the priests and Levites, who had responsibility for organizing the worship at the Temple, and the celebration of the main feasts of Passover, Weeks (Pentecost or *Shavuot*) and Tabernacles.

What would surprise us if we suddenly landed in Jerusalem early in the first century AD would be the sheer scale and size of the religious establishment. The population of Jerusalem was about 30,000 (except during the festivals when it virtually doubled in size) in a national population of some 500,000 in Judea.[22] There were in addition

---

22 Joachim Jeremias, *Jerusalem in the Time of Jesus* (London: SCM Press, 1969), pp. 205, 252.

approximately 16,000 male Scribes and Pharisees spread throughout the nation, and a further 17,000 priests and Levites who served in the Temple in rotas of duty.[23] As a rough estimate, one in five of the population would have been part of a religious institution (connected to either Scribes, Pharisees, Sadducees, priests or Levites). This far surpasses the numbers of religious as a proportion of the population in either medieval Christian society or Islam.

No wonder then that when an unknown, untrained preacher (in a formal religious sense) began preaching powerfully in the Spirit by the river Jordan, calling Israel to repentance and declaring the Pharisees and Sadducees a brood of vipers (Matthew 3:7), he caused a stir. Who was he? Where had he come from? What was his message? What authority did he have—from God or from men?[24] And so a "Commission of Enquiry" was sent down from Jerusalem to get answers to these and other questions.

A commission of enquiry

We are told that this "commission of enquiry", however formal or informal, was made up of priests, Levites and Pharisees (see John 1:19,24), and their business was to discover the identity of John the Baptist. Was he the Messiah himself, the one who was anointed to bring liberation and fulfilment to Israel? Was he Elijah returned, the one who had been taken up to heaven in a chariot at the end of his life and who had not died as an ordinary mortal (see 2 Kings 2:11,12). Indeed, there was a Jewish expectation that Elijah would return before the Messianic age, ushering in salvation and judgement. Malachi had prophesied, "See, I will send you the prophet Elijah before that great and dreadful day of the Lord comes" (Malachi 4:5). Was he the Prophet that Moses had spoken of in Deuteronomy 18:14 and following?

The Baptist standing there on the bank of the river Jordan, clothed in his trademark ascetic garments, refuses all three of these attributions. Even though the title "Messiah" is not directly mentioned by the

---

[23]   Jeremias, *Jerusalem in the Time of Jesus*, p. 204.

[24]   See Matthew 21:23–27; Mark 11:27–33; Luke 20:1–8.

Commission, knowing it to be present in everyone's minds, he quickly lays to one side such a thought. He does so, we are told, "freely", meaning he comes out with this confession (literally singleness of speech) off his own bat, without being prompted by a question. Nor is he Elijah, although later Jesus will say that the Baptist came in the spirit of Elijah: "If you are willing to accept it, he is the Elijah who was to come" (see Matthew 11:1–19, esp. verse 14). And nor is he the Prophet, this shadowy figure who is probably fulfilled in Jesus as Prophet, Priest and King. No, John is none of these three figures, and none of those titles can properly describe his role.

John the Baptist is instead, he says, "a voice of one crying in the desert, 'make straight the way of the Lord'" (Isaiah 40:3). Few renderings of these words better capture the thrill and excitement of this new beginning than the song of the same name in the 1973 musical *Godspell*. It is a *cry* marking a new epoch in human history, a new opportunity for Israel to make a fresh start. Indeed, the great prophetic chapter of Isaiah 40, which begins, "Comfort, comfort my people says your God", marks the end of exile and the start of a new era of salvation. Not content with this reply as an explanation of John's activity, the Pharisees press their enquiry by asking, "Why then do you baptize?" (John 1:24–25). John's answer in effect is that he is merely the warm-up act, or the spiritual *hors d'oeuvre* to the main course. To appreciate the main course, you must begin with the starter, which in spiritual terms is repentance demonstrated in baptism. Thus John, pointing to what is to come, says there is someone already in Israel to be revealed who is greater than he, so much greater in fact, that he, John, is not qualified even to do the work of a slave and untie his master's sandals (1:27). And to ground this, and so demonstrate that great theological insight was fixed for the Evangelist John in a specific time and place, the Evangelist tells us in passing that this all happened in another Bethany (for Bethany will be an important place name in John's narrative, see John 11:1). This other Bethany, unknown to us today, was on the far side of the Jordan, on the fringes of territorial Israel, and is not the Bethany near to Jerusalem, which was the village of Lazarus, Martha and Mary.

John's testimony increases expectation (1:29–34)

There are three fundamental activities that the Messiah, the Christ, will engage in, and two of them are spelt out in this section. First, directed by the Spirit, Jesus is identified by John the Baptist as the Lamb of God. The title most probably means the Lamb *provided by God*, whom we have already noted is also the Word and God himself (1:1). The Lamb of God is a phrase which recurs in many ways throughout Scripture. There is the lamb provided by God during Abraham's sacrifice of Isaac on Mount Moriah, which subsequently became the Temple mount (see Genesis 22:8 especially). There is the Passover lamb killed by the Israelites so that the Angel of Death will pass-over their households on the night of their release (Exodus 12, esp. verse 12). And there is the lamb led to the slaughter in Isaiah 53, from which the Servant of the Lord, fulfilled in time by Jesus, understands his own forthcoming sacrificial and redemptive death. All this and more is wrapped up in the Baptist's cry, "Look, the Lamb of God who takes away the sin of the world" (1:29). What is clear is that Jesus is the sacrifice for human sin; that he is provided by God and is himself God; and that he is a universal satisfaction for sin, since his self-offering will be a sacrifice for "the sin of the world".

Human sin is never hard to find, either on a grand scale or in its more banal form. To see sin rampant on a grand scale we have only to look at the present war in Ukraine: the bombing of civilians, the destruction of cities and human society, and the attempt at genocide. Or, more prosaically, we have sin operating in our own lives when we make poor choices, and in so doing fail to live up to the commandment to love God and neighbour. The French writer and sociologist Simone Weil put it this way: "Nothing is so beautiful and wonderful, nothing is so continually fresh and surprising, so full of sweet and perpetual ecstasy as the good. No desert is so dreary, monotonous, and boring as evil."[25] The point is that Jesus came as a sacrifice for the sin of the world, all of it in all time, and was the one through whom forgiveness could be found. This will

---

[25]   Quoted in Malcolm Muggeridge, *The Infernal Grove* (London: Collins Fontana, 1975), p. 145.

become the main theme of the Gospel from Chapter 12 onwards, when John unravels its significance and its meaning for Jesus.

Having identified Jesus as the Lamb of God and having said that Jesus was revealed to him during his general call to Israel to repent and be baptized—thus making John's baptism the curtain-raiser on Jesus's ministry—John then introduces Jesus as the bringer of the Spirit.

First, John says that he sees the Spirit come down upon Jesus as a dove (1:32), which is similar to the accounts in the Synoptic Gospels (see Matthew 3:16; Mark 1:10; Luke 3:22). The Spirit then remains (*ménō*) on him. "Remain" is a favourite word for John and Jesus, and John will use it in Chapter 15 in calling the branches (disciples) to *remain* in the vine (see 15:4). John the Baptist's recognition of Jesus as the Messiah and bringer of the Spirit comes about through the self-same Spirit who both directs him to start baptizing and also reveals the identity of Jesus (1:33). Jesus, the Baptist is told, will baptize not in water but in the Spirit.

In the course of these verses, which encapsulate the ministry and testimony of John the Baptist, we are told that Jesus is both the Lamb of God set forth as a sacrifice for human sin and the bringer of the Spirit. Both themes will run through the Gospel until the event of the crucifixion and the event of the risen Jesus breathing the Spirit upon the disciples in anticipation of Pentecost (20:22) fulfil the Baptist's predictions. The Baptist, as one of the seven great witnesses in the Gospel, could not have been more emphatic in his testimony than by concluding his introduction of Jesus with: "I have seen and I testify that this is the Son of God" (1:34, see also 1:6–9).

If John the Evangelist here sets out the two great roles of the Word made flesh—dealing with human sin and bringing the Spirit to the believers—he now moves to the third, which is building the Christian community.

The creation of the first Christian community (1:35–51)

No sooner is Jesus identified at his baptism (although that event is not specifically described in John's Gospel as it is in the others) than the process of building a new community based on discipleship begins. When Jesus is once again pointed out with the same words: "Look, the Lamb of God" (1:36), two disciples, Andrew and another—possibly John himself, who had already been drawn to the movement led by John the Baptist—overhear this exclamation and turn and begin following Jesus. Seeing them following him, Jesus asks what they want, and they try to respond by saying they want to go with him to his place (1:38). Jesus replies that they should come and see where he is staying (remaining). They arrive at 4 p.m., the tenth hour, and stay there, possibly even for the night.

We have no idea what they talked about. However, to be in the presence of Jesus for several hours, to see him at home, to be entertained by him and receive his hospitality, as was the way in the Middle East, must have been exhilarating. Whatever transpired, Andrew could not wait to find his brother Simon, tell him his conviction that "we have found the Messiah" (1:41b) and bring him to Jesus, whereupon Jesus, who seemingly already knows who Simon is, transfixes him with his gaze (*emblépō* = to fix one's gaze upon) and gives him a different name. The Aramaic name is Cephas, and the Greek name is Peter, meaning rock. And although in the Gospels Peter displays traits of impulsiveness, volatility, unreliability, and even foolhardiness, by the time of Pentecost he has become what Jesus called him: a rock. Jesus gathers others into this embryonic community as he moves north from Judea to Galilee. Another disciple, Philip, like Andrew and Simon Peter, comes from Bethsaida, a small town on the northern shores of Galilee which is to be castigated later for lack of repentance and faith, despite the many miracles performed there (Matthew 11:21; Luke 10:13). Like Andrew, Philip appears a natural evangelist, going to Nathanael and telling him, "We have found the one Moses wrote about in the Law and about whom the prophets also wrote" (1:45): the Messiah in other words. It is quite possible that Nathanael was a very close friend of Philip, with whom he had studied the Scriptures, asking the question as they did so, "When will the Messiah come?" Here, Philip believes, is their answer. There is only one snag: the Messiah comes from Nazareth. Nathanael, who comes from Cana (21:2) and seems something of a wit, regards Nazareth with disdain, famously saying, "Can anything good come from there?" The answer Philip gives is the same one Jesus gave to the earlier disciples, Andrew and possibly John, "Come and see" (1:39; 1:46b), which was a common rabbinic maxim. It proved effective.

When Jesus sees Nathanael, he makes two comments which convince him, or as we might say, blow him away! The first is insight into Nathanael's character, "Here is a true Israelite, in whom there is nothing false" (1:47). Nathanael's name literally means "Gift of God" in Hebrew, but Jesus discerns a character entirely straightforward and without guile. Astonished at such an immediate and accurate psychometric assessment, Nathanael's swift response is, "How do you know me?" (1:48). Jesus gives further proof of his supernatural knowledge by saying he even knew Nathanael's movements just before Philip came along to tell him of his discovery: he was sitting under a fig tree. This is enough. Nathanael then comes out with the most emphatic confession, "Rabbi, you are the Son of God; you are the King of Israel" (1:49). In the Synoptic Gospels, it takes Simon Peter well into the Galilean ministry and before Jesus turns to go to Jerusalem to make a similar confession (Matthew 16:16; Mark 8:29; Luke 9:20). Jesus's response to Nathanael's amazement at his knowledge is, in effect, "You have not seen anything yet." Jesus's saying about "the angels of God ascending and descending on the Son of Man" (1:51) is most likely a figure of speech, which means that Jesus will bring the realities of heaven to earth through his words and actions. As Jacob saw this in a dream (Genesis 28:10–15), now Jesus will make it a reality on earth. It is the closing sentence to this episode, which could only have further increased expectation. Nathanael is not chosen to be an Apostle, but he will stick close by Jesus, and is in the boat fishing with the other disciples at the end of the Gospel (see 21:2).

The creation, and indeed the growth, of this embryonic Christianity is full of lessons for evangelism. Thus, of Paul's writings, from Romans to Philemon, it is fair to say that "they embody in their own situational purposes the overall aim, not of communication merely, but of community".[26] Two principles are clear. The first is the invitation, *to come and see* where Jesus is staying, made to Andrew and possibly to Andrew's companion, John himself (1:39). The invitation is then made to Nathanael to also *come and see* Jesus for himself (1:46b). In other words, evangelism happens by inviting others to local Christian gatherings where people can see for themselves that our communities are places where people can encounter Jesus, learn more about themselves and God's call on their lives, and where love and truth will surround them.

Secondly, the example of Andrew and Philip in *bringing* Simon and Nathanael to Jesus demonstrates that they not only told others that they had found the Messiah, but they then *brought them* to Jesus, making the introduction themselves. It is through these connections, and through these very human means of inviting and bringing, that the Kingdom of God grows.

By the end of this first chapter, not only has the Baptist made plain through his witness that Jesus is both the Lamb of God and the bringer to his people of the third member of the Trinity, the Holy Spirit, but that Jesus is also the founder of a new community which will grow and grow through the Gospel in the face of heated opposition. Indeed, in this first remarkable chapter, Jesus is depicted as the Word made flesh, the Light of the World, the only begotten of the Father, the Messiah, the Lord (1:23), the Lamb of God, the Baptizer with the Spirit, and the Son of God (1:49). No other Gospel writer has a more exalted view of Christ from the very beginning: he is of cosmic authority and eternal significance, and yet has intimate knowledge of each person.

---

[26] N. T. Wright, *Paul and the Faithfulness of God* (London: SPCK, 2013), Part IV, p. 1476.

CHAPTER 3

New Wine in Israel

John 2:1–25

At first glance, and maybe at second glance also, it looks as though the first of the seven signs in the Gospel, the changing of the water into wine at the wedding of Cana in Galilee and the cleansing of the Temple, have little to do with each other, but perhaps they do. Furthermore, these two events taken together may be a striking example of the chord struck in the final part of the overture which is the Prologue of the Gospel, in laying out the themes that are to be developed. The words in the Prologue which are of particular interest in connection with John 2 are these:

> From the fullness of his grace we have all received one blessing after another. For the Law was given through Moses: grace and truth came through Jesus Christ.
>
> *John 1:16–17*

The point is that at the beginning of the Gospel, John sets out to show how this is true in the actions and words of Jesus the Messiah. To put it at its simplest, he comes to bring a fresh start to Israel; to fulfil all that Moses promised and pointed to in his teaching; to bring grace in succession to Law; and to replace the emptiness of Judaism and its corrupt worship—as evidenced in the Temple—with the grace and truth of the gospel. If this is right, we can see how the cleansing of the Temple and the changing of water into wine hold together.

The changing of water into wine (2:1–12)

The account begins with the memorable phrase, "On the third day". At one level, this recalls the day of resurrection, which was the most fundamental transformation in human history. At a more everyday level, it builds on the sequence used in the previous chapter, in which five previous days are specified (1:1–28; 1:29–34; 1:35–39; 1:40–42 (assumed) and 1:43–51). Together these days, along with a day of rest, echo the first creation week of Genesis. Thus, the third day after this sequence means the eighth day. Following this sequence there is no more counting of days in the Gospel. Thus in 2:12 John simply recalls, "After this he went down to Capernaum."

On this *third day*, or we might say, at the beginning of a new working week, Jesus is found with his mother and his disciples at a wedding in Cana of Galilee. It is often assumed that it was a family wedding on Mary's side of the family, as she appears keenly involved in its smooth functioning. The wedding, which often could last up to three days, is proceeding well until a fateful comment is made by his mother to Jesus: "They have no more wine" (2:3). This would have heralded a socially disastrous turn of events for the hosting family, which at this stage appears to be the groom's family.

Weddings in first-century Middle Eastern societies were not simply celebrations of the love of two individuals, but the coming together of two families. Honour was not far from the thoughts of each family: the honour to both families from presenting a bride who was a virgin; the honour that each family bestowed on each other; and the honour bestowed on the couple by the guests, their presence, and their gifts. "To run out of food or wine at a wedding involved a serious loss of family honour. It signalled not only a lack of financial resources, but even more a lack of friends. In order to avoid such embarrassment and ensure a wedding that brought a family public honour, associations were formed among village men for the purpose of mutual assistance (referred sometimes as the sons of the bridal chamber, see Mark 2:19)."[27] The bride

---

[27]   Bruce Malina and Richard Rohrbaugh, *Social Science Commentary on the Gospel of St John* (Minneapolis: Fortress, 1989), p. 70.

would be washed, perfumed and dressed by her bridesmaids, who would then go ahead and wait at the groom's house, as in the parable of the wise and foolish bridesmaids (Matthew 25:1–13). The groom would bring his bride to his home with a procession of dancing and music and then feast there. Perhaps it was at this point that they ran out of wine, at the height and culmination of the celebrations. What greater let-down could there be than having no more to drink! What greater embarrassment for the groom! What comments would fly around the village about the wedding where the wine ran out! How inauspicious for the prospects of the marriage.

Mary's words, "They have no more wine", may be taken at many levels, as is typical with John. Her words are both literal and symbolic, human and spiritual, for the moment and for all time. Firstly, it is a literal fact that they have no more wine in the bottles or jars in which it was contained. They are plain empty. Not enough wine has been laid by. The host has underestimated the drinking. But secondly, it is a statement about Judaism. From its inception when God spoke to Abraham through to the giving of the Law to Moses, through the long years of disobedience, exile and restoration, Judaism had waxed and waned. Now in Jesus's day it had become a heavy burden imposed by the religiously zealous on a weary and harassed people.[28] Judaism was empty: "They have no more wine."

Finally, the words "they have no more wine" can resonate with our own lives. They can be a commentary about us. We too can easily be depleted of spiritual resources and face a real spiritual emptiness from many causes. During the bleak times of the pandemic, one brave professor wrote of her losses: "Goodbye Mum, you died of Covid 19 days before you were due to be vaccinated. You told them to give the ventilator to someone else. I said a Facetime farewell from a hospital car park. You will have a Zoom Funeral. You are 2020. But thanks to the devoted, exhausted, NHS Staff."[29] Further back, in 1942, the journalist and then MI6 agent Malcolm Muggeridge, working in Maputo (Lorenzo Marques)

---

28 See Matthew 23:13–39 on the woes to the Pharisees and teachers of the Law, and Matthew 9:36 on Jesus, "When he saw the crowds, he had compassion on them, because they were . . . like sheep without a shepherd."

29 Trisha Greenhalgh, "My Covid Year", *The Times*, 2 July 2021.

in Mozambique of all places, fell into a dark mood from which there seemed no escape. He resolved to take his own life by swimming out to sea, only to be summoned by a cross-shaped light shining through the barred window of a café called Peter's in Costa da Sol. He recalled:

> Though I scarcely realized it at the time and subsequently only very slowly and dimly, this episode represented for me one of those deep changes which take place in our lives ... Thenceforth all my values and pursuits were going to undergo a total transformation—from the carnal to the spiritual; from the immediate, the now, towards the everlasting, the eternal. In a tiny dark dungeon of the ego, chained and manacled, I had glimpsed a glimmer of light coming in through a barred window high above me. It was the light of Peter's Café and Costa da Sol calling me back to earth, my mortal home; it was the grey light of morning heralding another day as I floundered and struggled through the black mud; it was the Light of the world. The bars of the window as I looked closely, took on the form of a Cross.[30]

Our own experiences of mistakes or failure, a seeming interminable struggle with a health issue, a loss of work, or the break-up of a close relationship, can lead to a sense in ourselves of there being "no more wine".

Jesus's response to the literal fact that "they have no more wine" is, on the face of it, not very encouraging. He replies to his mother, "Woman"— although translated more softly by the NIV as "dear woman"—with the words "Why do you involve me? My time (hour) has not yet come" (2:4). It is an intriguing reply since Jesus's public ministry has begun with his baptism and appearance with John the Baptist. He has already been recognized as the Lamb of God, the Son of God, and the Messiah. Surely the time for secrecy or hiding his identity has passed? But the phrase "my hour" is better than the translation "my time", as it conveys greater precision, a *kairos* or crisis moment, and it has an almost technical role in the Gospel, referring to his time of glorification or passion. Thus, in

---

30   Muggeridge, *The Infernal Grove*, p. 204.

John 7:6,8,30 and 8:20, Jesus again says his time, or the hour, has not come. But then in John 12:23 he says emphatically, "The time (or hour) *has come* for the Son of Man to be glorified." Perhaps Jesus is reluctant to be drawn into this his first sign, revealing, as we are told, his glory (2:11b), because it brings home the inevitable path to his passion and redemptive sufferings when his true nature and destiny will be revealed to his own great cost.

Whatever Jesus has in mind, Mary is not put off and nor does Jesus fail to act to relieve this unusual need. Mary says to the servants (or catering team), "Do whatever he tells you" (2:5). It is another of those sayings with significance, both for that moment and for all time. Jesus commands the servants to fill the purification jars—holding about 100 litres apiece—to the brim with water. Then the servants are to draw off the water, and, as etiquette requires, take it to the "master of the banquet" or the *maître d'hôtel*.

The master of ceremonies pronounces the verdict on the miracle-cum-parable. So flabbergasted is he by this wine that he buttonholes the bridegroom in the full flight of the festivities, saying, "Everyone brings out the choice wine first and then cheaper wine after the guests have had too much to drink; but you have saved the best till now" (2:10). This is true of this sign or miracle itself, that the quality of this new wine is exceptional, and the quantity prodigious—some 600 bottles! But more importantly, it is instructive at a far deeper spiritual level also. The old wine represents the Law, which has served its purpose, and which can condemn but not save (see Romans 3:20). The Law is now empty of salvific power and has been replaced, good though it was (see Paul's argument in Romans 7:1–12), superseded by grace, i.e., unmerited forgiveness and adoption, which can transform, change and equip. Grace is the new wine, exceptional and available in unlimited quantities. Those who taste it, and who will taste it, are sure of its surpassing vintage. As John says in his Prologue, "From the fullness of his grace we have all received one blessing after another. For the Law was given through Moses: grace and truth came through Jesus the Messiah" (1:16,17). The rest of the Gospel will be an exposition of that grace at work.

If we had to imagine the first sign that the Word Incarnate would perform when on earth, we might be hard pushed to imagine that it would be the creation of 600 bottles of wine of the very best vintage for a wedding party that may have already drunk too much! And yet on reflection, there is a symmetry and a revelation about this miracle or sign. It is not just about the power of the Word to transform water into wine and all that signifies spiritually. It depicts the overwhelming generosity, quality and purpose of God's provision. At the end of time, there will be a wedding of the Lamb to his Church, described as a city, a New Jerusalem, dressed as a bride (see Revelation 19:6–8; 21:2). Surely the Wedding at Cana is a foretaste of that eschatological event? No wonder, as the editor of the Gospel of John said, "He [Jesus] thus revealed his glory and [consequently] his disciples put their faith in him" (2:11b). Presumably they too had a glass of the wine, and in time heard how it had been made. Following this first sign we are told Jesus, his family and the disciples go back to Capernaum, on the west side of Galilee, and stay there for a few days (2:12).

The cleansing of the Temple (2:13–25)

We might justifiably ask why the Wedding at Cana and the Cleansing of the Temple appear in the same section or chapter. One answer could simply be that they are chronologically close together, as the text suggests (see 2:12,13). However, there could be a deeper reason too, which is that both the Wedding at Cana, with the changing of water into wine, and the Cleansing of the Temple demonstrate the need for transformation and renewal in Israel, and John sees them as one of a piece.

Before looking at the Cleansing of the Temple in greater detail, we must acknowledge that John has placed this event at the start of his Gospel, while the three Synoptic Gospels have it in the final week of Jesus's earthly life (see Matthew 21:12ff.; Mark 11:15–17; and Luke 19:45ff.). Either John has deliberately chosen to place it at the beginning for a theological reason, or there were in fact two very similar occasions. The simple truth is that we shall never know on this earth. However, there is good reason theologically for placing it here, based on an understanding that it again demonstrates the emptiness of Judaism and the corruption of temple worship.

The history of the Temple in Israel's life is frequently problematic. Originally Israel had been instructed to build a Tabernacle, which was to be at the centre of their worship (Exodus 26). It was a moveable centre, with an Ark containing the Law below a mercy seat and flanked with two golden cherubim. Here God would make his presence known (see also Exodus 40, the glory of the Lord in the Tabernacle). Inside the inner sanctuary and near the Ark, which was shielded by a curtain, were the altar of incense symbolizing the prayer of Israel, the table for the shewbread, the menorah, and the altar for the burnt offerings. The Ark and the Temple were symbols of heaven touching earth, and of earth reaching up to heaven—nothing less. Attending the Temple were priests taken from the family of Aaron, and Levites, both appointed to oversee the organization of the worship. This form of worship sufficed for the better part of a thousand years, until King David and his son Solomon conceived of a permanent Temple. Solomon's Temple, a most magnificent building, was built with no expense spared, and at its inauguration was filled with the glory of the Lord (1 Kings 8). But soon the Northern Kingdom of Israel and the Southern Kingdom of Judah came to rely for their confidence before God on the edifice of the Temple, rather than on holy living according to the Law (see Jeremiah 7:4). Eventually, when a new low point was reached and pagan deities were worshipped in the Temple, God's presence departed (see Ezekiel 10). After being besieged by the Babylonians, the elite remnant was taken into exile (597 BC) where they heard of the final destruction of Solomon's Temple and of Jerusalem (586 BC), following a rebellion against Babylonian rule (see Ezekiel 33:21ff.).

After the return from exile and under the inspiration of the prophets Haggai and Zechariah, and the leadership of Ezra and Zerubbabel (see Ezra 3), a second Temple was constructed in the sixth century BC and completed in 516. Compared with its predecessor it was a modest structure, and it was not until the arrival of Herod the Great (37–4 BC) that a huge rebuilding plan got underway, of which the Western Wailing Wall is the only structure left standing today. Nevertheless, the Temple remained the great symbol of Israel's future hope, the place where heaven and earth met in worship, and where the eschatological hopes of Israel would find expression.[31]

By the start of Jesus's ministry, the rebuilding of the Temple had been underway for 46 years (see 2:20). Up to 18,000 workmen were said to be working on the building.[32] It is this Temple, so recently rebuilt and finished, that Jesus now enters on that fateful day during the Feast of Passover, with Jerusalem teeming with pilgrims from the Diaspora for the great Jewish feast—seemingly the first Passover of Jesus's three-year ministry. What confronts Jesus when he enters is a market: cattle, sheep and doves being sold for sacrifice, and money being changed from Roman coinage into Temple coinage with an unhealthy mark up. It had become a money-making machine in which the true worship of prayer and sacrifice was exchanged for profit. The Temple had lost its way and Jesus shows his distress and anger at the exploitation of his Father's house by overturning the tables and driving out the traders and their animals with a whip of cord in his hand.

Asked for signs of his authority for this action, Jesus says provocatively, "Destroy this temple, and I will raise it again in three days" (2:19). In an editorial comment, John tells us that he is speaking about his own body, which he describes as a Temple (2:21). His resurrection body, and then the Church, will become the new Temple inhabited by the Spirit. Indeed, with the destruction of the Temple in AD 70 by the legions of Titus, the Church, now including Jew and Gentile, will become the successor to the Jerusalem Temple, the place in which the living God might be worshipped on the basis of Jesus's completed sacrifice of himself. The Apostle Peter will make this clear in his own writings (see 1 Peter 2:4ff.).

In this chapter, John intends to show us that the Incarnate Word has come to renew Israel. The first sign at Cana is not only a miracle of transformation showing the Messiah's power, but also a parable that he has come to refill the empty jars of Judaism, as well as our own impoverished spirituality, with new and remarkable wine. But this renewal comes at a cost. There must be a turning away from exploitation and abuse towards genuine worship, so that God may truly indwell his people. And although

---

[31]   See Tom Wright, *Paul: A Biography* (London: SPCK, 2018), p. 20.

[32]   See Jeremias, *Jerusalem in the Time of Jesus*, p. 22.

many believe in the Messiah during that Passover (2:23), he is not so naïve as to think that his path will henceforward be strewn with flowers. He knows that in the end a crown of thorns awaits him (2:24). Once more the editor interjects to say that the Son of Man knows the depths to which humans can descend (2:25).

New Birth

John 3:1–36

We come here to one of the best-known chapters of John's Gospel, a chapter that has given rise to the idea of spiritual new birth. Yet taken as a whole, it is a chapter that contrasts two men: the one enquiring, seeking and tentatively exploring—Nicodemus; the other proclaiming, baptizing and teaching—John the Baptist. Although they appear in the same chapter, they are rarely compared and contrasted. But what both men learn is that full faith is the product of the work of the Father, the Son and the Holy Spirit. And to this end, we hear the voices of Nicodemus, Jesus, John the Baptist and the Apostle John himself woven together. They make up two conversations, and within and around them is the first discourse of the Gospel.

The teacher who came by night (3:1–21)

If in the previous chapter Jesus confronts and cleanses one of the great institutions of Judaism, the Temple—the place where heaven and earth meet in holy worship—in this chapter Jesus confronts the other great pillar of Jewish faith, the Law or Torah, and its self-appointed guardians: the Scribes and Pharisees. In Nicodemus, we have one of the élite of Jerusalem, a Pharisee, well instructed and taught, and zealous for the Jewish Law. The name Pharisee literally means "the separate ones" or "the holy ones of Israel".[33] They had been part of Israel since the second century

---

[33] Jeremias, *Jerusalem in the Time of Jesus*, p. 246.

BC. The Scribes were a different group, but often the more instructed Pharisees were also Scribes, only not all. Not only was Nicodemus a Pharisee, he was also a member of the ruling Jewish Council of Jerusalem, the Sanhedrin. The Sanhedrin was a group of 71 elders of the people, first established after the return from exile.[34] This Council comprised the Chief Priests, some Scribes, and the elders of the people, who were a kind of lay nobility. It was a court and aristocratic senate, able to rule in matters of Law and Jewish affairs. Nicodemus was such a man: one of the principal men of the city. He comes by night to see Jesus, and so begins one of the most memorable conversations in the Gospel.

Nicodemus's opening gambit in his conversation with Jesus is nothing if not diplomatic. He has, it seems, been drawn by Jesus's teaching and demeanour to seek Jesus out and discover more about the person behind the "signs" that have so impressed him. "Rabbi", he calls Jesus—although Jesus has had no formal rabbinic training—"We know that you are a teacher who has come from God. For no one could perform the signs you are doing if God were not with him" (3:2). Nicodemus's enquiry is respectful, tentative, diplomatic and non-committal. He seeks more evidence from the lips of Jesus so that he might discern how he should be regarded. In response to this almost hedge-betting approach, Jesus comes out with one of his emphatic, no room for fudging or equivocations, replies. It is preceded by the attention-grabbing phrase, "Very truly", which appears throughout the Gospel whenever Jesus wants to give a seminal piece of teaching. Here he tells Nicodemus, "No one can see the Kingdom of God unless they are born again" (3:3).

At the heart of Jesus's teaching is the Kingdom of God, although the phrase occurs very seldom in John's Gospel. It reappears in Chapter 18, recording the trial before Pilate, in which Jesus says to the Roman Governor, "My Kingdom is not of this world. If it were, my servants would fight to prevent my arrest by the Jewish leaders. But now my Kingdom is from another place" (18:36). On two occasions in this Gospel when speaking to people of power and influence (and in Pilate's case, earthly power over Jesus's own life) Jesus chooses to speak of his Kingdom. It is unseen, from another place, and is the *final reality* in the power structures

---

[34] Jeremias, *Jerusalem in the Time of Jesus*, p. 222.

of the universe. Entrance into this Kingdom, of which his miracles are a sign, is by a second birth. This is the only place in the Scriptures where Jesus uses this metaphor to clarify how any may truly enter his Kingdom.

Understandably, Nicodemus is mystified. How can a human be born a second time? Can he re-enter his mother's womb and be thus born again?"

Jesus explains to Nicodemus that this second birth, which leads to entry into the Kingdom of God, can only come about through water and the Spirit: "Flesh gives birth to flesh, but the Spirit gives birth to spirit" (3:6). The point is that to enter this new sphere of existence, which is the Kingdom of God, two things are required: water and the Spirit. Water picks up on the process of birth, i.e., the breaking of waters, and also symbolizes repentance through baptism; while the Spirit himself, the third member of the Trinity, must also be at work in this process.

For the first time in the Gospel, we are introduced to the work of the Spirit, in contrast to being told by John the Baptist that Jesus is the bringer of the Spirit (1:33). The Word and the Father have been introduced from the outset. Jesus is the Incarnate Word who is God (1:1) and is variously described as the Messiah (Christ) and the Son of Man. Now Jesus introduces the Spirit as wind or breath. The background to this metaphor must be the Old Testament, and in particular the passage in Ezekiel where God gives life to dry bones in response to the prophet's word of command (see Ezekiel 37:1–14). Indeed, in the New Testament the Spirit is often likened to breath or wind. At Pentecost, the Spirit is symbolized by "a rushing mighty wind" (Acts 2:2), and at the end of the Gospel, Jesus anticipates the gift of the Spirit in the Church by breathing on the Apostles and saying, "receive the Holy Spirit" (John 20:22). Jesus makes the point that, as with the wind, you can see evidence of the Spirit's presence, but you cannot actually see the Spirit himself. Thus, "the wind blows wherever it pleases. You hear its sound, but you cannot tell where it comes from or where it is going. So it is with everyone born of the Spirit" (3:8).

Such teaching about the Spirit and the new birth is news to Nicodemus. In astonishment he asks, "How can this be?" (3:9). And with equal astonishment, but perhaps not altogether surprised, Jesus replies, "You are Israel's teacher, and do you not understand these things?" Such teaching may come as a surprise to many today. For Christianity is not primarily about observing a moral code, or going frequently to church, but is instead about exercising faith in Christ and receiving the Spirit's work in our lives. This was something for Nicodemus to come to terms with. After all, he had been trained since his youth to observe the Torah in all its parts so that he might become one of the righteous in Israel and so find God's favour. Here is something new. Jesus says he needs a *new beginning, a new birth*, that must be brought about through the Spirit. This "testimony" or "witness" (see 3:11, Greek *marturían* from which we derive the word "martyr") which Jesus is imparting to a somewhat bewildered Nicodemus—turning all his preconceptions upside down—is based on Jesus's personal knowledge. It is prefigured in the Prologue, where John tells us that "to all who received him, to those who believed in his name, he gave the right to become children of God—children *born* not of natural descent, nor of human decision or a husband's will, *but born of God*" (John 1:12–13). (We might add being born of the Father, the Son and the Spirit.) What Jesus teaches here is knowledge taken from heaven and now given on earth (3:11–13).

Jesus then asks, somewhat dismissively of Nicodemus's understanding, what chance there is of him understanding more heavenly teaching, if he cannot grasp what Jesus is presently saying. Not content with having revolutionized Nicodemus's perspective by declaring observance of the Law is not enough (see Romans 3:20), Jesus throws into the conversation another sublime truth which Nicodemus will not grasp, but which will make him deeply ponder.

Using an illustration taken from the wanderings of Israel in the desert as recorded in the book of Numbers (21:4–9), Jesus now explains the significance of his own death. If the Spirit is responsible for bringing Nicodemus, or any believer for that matter, into new birth—enabling them to see and enter the Kingdom of God—the death of Jesus will make this possible by removing any hindrance caused by the deadly bite of sin. Thus, Jesus goes on to explain that the Son of Man (his favourite title for himself, taken from Daniel) will, like the bronze snake in the Numbers story, be lifted up to forgive all who look with faith on his death. In Numbers 21, the Israelites have been punished for their rebellion against Moses and God and for their complaints about being brought into the desert and deprived of a varied menu. Many have been punished for this by snake bites, but a cure is then offered by God in the form of a bronze snake, indeed a replica of those snakes that have attacked them, then pinned to a pole so that any who look upon it will be healed. The implication is that Jesus will himself become like the cause of human injury and death, that is sin itself, and in so doing relieve all those with faith from the deadly effects of the venom (see 2 Corinthians 5:21).

It is a powerful illustration. The story would have been well known to Nicodemus. It is rich with imagery of the snake and the fall of humankind due to the serpent's work in the paradise of Eden (see Genesis 3:1–7). It involves Jesus becoming like the thing from which humanity needs saving. The Apostle Paul puts it succinctly in Corinthians where he writes, "God made him who had no sin to be sin for us, so that in him we might become the righteousness of God" (2 Corinthians 5:21). It is a lot for Nicodemus to take in at one sitting, and as with most of Jesus's teaching about his death before the event, it is only understood in retrospect. Furthermore, John, as the editor and author, reckons it will be difficult for his readership to understand, so he adds what is to my mind the most famous editorial comment in the Scriptures.

Although some biblical translations continue to set John 3:16–21 in quotation marks (which, like all punctuation marks, do not exist in the original), as if Jesus is speaking, the style of the speech referring to the Lord as God rather than Father and the general tone of editorial reflection make it much more likely this most famous passage is the reflection of the Evangelist rather than the direct speech of Jesus. The passage divides into two: a reflection on the significance of the Cross and a reflection on the metaphor, so beloved of John, of light and darkness.

John's reflection on the Cross, about which Jesus has just been speaking to Nicodemus in the illustration of the serpent in the wilderness, centres on the ideas of love, gift and belief. The motivation for his giving is love. We are told famously that "God so loved the world that he gave his one and only Son, that whoever believes in him shall not perish but have eternal life" (3:16). Furthermore, we are told that God did not send his Son into the world to condemn the world, but to save the world through him (3:17). Love is the essence of God, along with light, the two forming John's fundamental description of the nature of God (see 1 John 1:5 and 1

John 4:16b). It is between these twin poles, this axis of God's being, that God's response to human waywardness is found. God's love precipitates his giving: a giving of the Father and a giving of the Son, as told in the second part of this Gospel (from John 12 onwards) which concentrates on the exaltation and glorification of the Son in his passion. The intention of this giving is to offer the world—meaning all people hitherto living in ignorance or opposition to God—eternal life, and hence remove them from a place of condemnation and judgement. What they must do is believe, trust and have faith, and they will enjoy salvation and escape judgement (3:18).

Judgement is a strong theme in the Gospel. It seems to be both an eschatological fact (i.e., a final event) but also a present reality. In the Gospel, Jesus is the judge (see 5:22,23,30; 8:16,26) and there is a future judgement (5:28–29). Furthermore, in the here and now people's reactions to Jesus are present judgement (9:39–41). If judgement is a reality both in the present and in the future, removal from its condemnation comes, says John, through faith in the Son of Man (3:18). When as an older man Michelangelo (1475–1564) painted the final scene of the Last Judgement in the Sistine Chapel, some 25 years after he completed the famous ceiling, it is said that he had doubts about his own spiritual destiny despite his belief, and this is evident in this painting. Thus, Michelangelo paints himself into the picture to the right of Christ, flayed but with his face visible, and held up by St Bartholomew. Michelangelo might have gained more confidence of salvation had he heeded John's words here. However, John makes it clear that belief in the Son is the basis of freedom from judgement or condemnation (see Romans 8:1), and to believe means we may have confidence in the future. Our lives may be assessed, but we are free from condemnation.

The second theme in John's reflection on this conversation with Nicodemus concerns darkness and light. Once again this takes up the theme first stated in the Prologue, where John tells us, "The light shines in the darkness, and the darkness has not overcome it" (1:5). John begins this later reflection by saying, "this is the verdict" (literally the *krisis*), that the process of judgement is underway, for the coming of light into the world has divisive effects. Those with evil in their hearts and whose deeds are evil refuse to come to the light because their evil deeds will be exposed for what they are, while those who have endeavoured to live by the truth will recognize the light and come to it (3:19–21). In other words, the presence of the light in the world brings about a crisis—a process that will have its culmination on the day of judgement. In the meantime, light attracts those who seek goodness and repels those who orchestrate evil. It was the great Russian author Aleksandr Solzhenitsyn (1918–2008) who wrote, "Gradually it was disclosed to me that the line separating good and evil passes not through states, nor between classes, not between political parties either, but right through every human heart and through all hearts. It is impossible to expel evil from the world in its entirety, but it is possible to constrict it within each person."[35]

Testimony of John the Baptist and a further reflection (3:22–36)

As with the conversation with Nicodemus, which is followed by a reflection by the Evangelist John (3:16–21), so now an exchange with John the Baptist is followed by a further reflection from the Evangelist (3:31–36). The context for this conversation between the Baptist and some of his disciples is a faintly competitive spirit about baptism. John's disciples are concerned about who is baptizing most, the Baptist or Jesus and his disciples. At this point, John is baptizing at a place where there is a lot of water, an unlocated spot called Aenon, with seven springs nearby.[36] A rumour has reached the Baptist's disciples that Jesus and his disciples are baptizing more people, although we learn later that Jesus is not himself baptizing at all (4:2). The disciples of the Baptist are further tipped off balance by a seemingly arcane argument with a Jew about ceremonial washing, although we are not told exactly what this Jew's point is (see also Mark 7:5). They then come with their questions to John

---

35   Aleksandr Solzhenitsyn, *The Gulag Archipelago* (London: Collins, 1974–8), p. 253.

36   Leon Morris, *Gospel According to St John* (London: Marshall, Morgan and Scott, 1973), p. 273.

the Baptist, who gives a majestic reply that includes some memorable words.

In answer to their implicit question about the relative authority and success of himself and Jesus, John the Baptist is anxious to dispel any residual myths about him being the Messiah and instead exalt the authority and scope of Jesus's ministry. First, he says that the extent and limits of his own ministry have been clearly determined by heaven (3:27). He reiterates what he said in Chapter 1, that he is not the Christ (1:20). Indeed, as the Prologue makes clear, "He himself was not the light; he came only as a witness to the light" (1:8). Then, in another metaphor, John describes himself as the friend of the bridegroom, who delights in hearing the bridegroom's voice and listens out carefully for him (3:29). John then says that his joy is now complete because the bridegroom is here, and his voice may be heard. He ends with the memorable sentence: "He must become greater [increase] and I must become less [decrease]" (3:30). This sentiment serves as a model for all disciples of Jesus, in fact—our ego must serve his purposes in our lives and our likeness to him increase.

The final section of the chapter (3:31–36) is most probably a further editorial reflection by the Evangelist on the relative importance of the Baptist and Jesus. John makes a distinction between the man from heaven (Jesus) and the man from earth (John the Baptist, or indeed any disciple). The point is that the heavenly man (Jesus, or the Word made flesh) far surpasses the earthly, for "the one who comes from heaven is above all" (3:31). By contrast, the earthly person is limited by his origins in understanding and power. Nevertheless, when the heavenly man speaks or acts, many do not accept his testimony, while those who do accept what he says show that they recognize and affirm the truth. Once again, the Evangelist John makes it clear that the one who receives the witness or testimony (*marturían*) of Jesus who is "the one from heaven" will discover that God is truthful (3:33). Furthermore, in an interesting Trinitarian verse, Jesus, as the one whom God the Father has sent, speaks the words of the Father because he has been given the Spirit without measure (3:34). All members of the Trinity are fully involved in making God known on earth. The verse (3:34) demonstrates once again the intertwining of the Trinity—the Father, Son and Spirit—in a common objective of making known God himself, through the Son being sent by the Father, and the Son also being immeasurably filled by the Spirit. One of the great early-Church teachers on the Trinity put it like this: "All that the Father is we see revealed in the Son; all that is the Son's is the Father's also; for the whole Son dwells in the Father, and has the whole Father dwelling in him. The Son who exists always in the Father can never be separated from him, nor can the Spirit ever be divided from the Son who through the Spirit works all things. He who receives the Father also receives at the same time the Son and Spirit."[37] To that John would have surely said "Amen". John adds a final piece of editorial insight, saying, "the Father loves the Son and has placed everything in his hands" and therefore "any who believes in the Son has life, but those who reject the Son are still subject to God's wrath [Greek: *òrgē*]" (3:36).

Taken as a whole, the chapter is a revelation of how Jesus brings salvation. He explains the process to Nicodemus, who, for all his eminence, is an infant when it comes to understanding the ways of the Kingdom. In his first reflection (3:16–21), John the Evangelist underlines the offer of God, motivated by love but requiring belief to be effective (3:18). John the Baptist adds his voice, exalting the testimony of Jesus as the heavenly man, and then, in a further reflection (3:31–36), the Evangelist tells his readers once again that our response must be to believe (3:36). There is no missing the imperative of his Gospel.

---

[37]   Gregory of Nyssa, cited by Kallistos Ware, *The Orthodox Way* (Crestwood, NY: SVS Press, 1979), p. 31.

CHAPTER 5

The Water of Life

John 4:1–42

The conversation with the Samaritan woman must be one of the most delightful narratives in Scripture. It is unique to John's Gospel, just as the Parable of the Prodigal Son is unique to Luke's. Without either of them our understanding of Jesus and his mission would be greatly diminished. For John, the event is a marvellous example of the grace and truth of Jesus being demonstrated in mission. And once again one of the statements of the Prologue—"the Law was given through Moses; grace and truth came through Jesus Christ"—is fulfilled in action by Jesus. We see both *grace and truth* at play in this vivid and extraordinary meeting.

John vividly sets the scene. Jesus is travelling back from Judea, possibly from Aenon near Salim, north of Jericho on the west side of the Jordan, to Galilee.[38] To get there, Jesus has to pass through Samaria and close to Mount Gerizim, which is a little south of Sebaste or the city of Samaria and Shechem. At about midday (the sixth hour), a tired and weary Jesus sits down beside a well once dug by Jacob (Genesis 33:18–20).

While Jesus is seated there, a Samaritan woman comes out at midday to draw water. When she approaches, Jesus addresses her, and in so doing breaks two conventions: speaking to a woman in public, particularly one with her history as it transpires, and talking with a Samaritan, with whom Jews had no dealings (4:9b).

Samaritans were a hybrid people. They originated as part of the Northern Kingdom of Israel, which had had its capital at Samaria and its religious centres at Bethel, Dan and Shechem (1 Kings 12:25ff.), while

---

[38] *Oxford Bible Atlas* (Oxford: Oxford University Press, 1974), p. 86.

its territory included the tribal lands of Ephraim and Western Manasseh. The area had been overwhelmed by the Assyrians in 722 BC and was resettled by varied peoples taken from the Assyrian empire (2 Kings 17:24ff.), along with their own customs of worship (see 2 Kings 17:29). This ethnic and religious mix caused Jews to despise Samaritans as a mongrel race with only a loose attachment to Judaism. Nevertheless, Jesus speaks to this woman, and proceeds to offer her, although in different terms, the same hope he does to the elite ruler Nicodemus in Jerusalem. In so doing, Jesus indicates that the Church, or the called-out ones who are becoming his followers, are an extraordinary cross-section of people.

Grace leads

The grace of Jesus is evident from his opening words. He crosses barriers. He overturns conventions. He reaches out to this lonely and seemingly shunned woman. Reaching out to people who are different from ourselves is a sure sign of grace. Archbishop Desmond Tutu (1931–2021), who was affectionately known as "the Arch", had a profoundly important role in South Africa, both in ending apartheid and in seeking reconciliation through the Truth and Reconciliation Commission. His family's faith was engendered by the ministry of Archbishop Trevor Huddleston (1913–88), who frequently doffed his hat to Desmond's mother in Sophiatown, showing respect across the racial divide. When Tutu was ill, Huddleston visited him in hospital and became the single greatest influence of Tutu's life. It began with gracious actions.

Jesus's gracious opening words in which he asks for a drink from this unnamed woman soon develop into a conversation which comes close to conversational repartee. There are several occasions in the Gospels where Jesus encounters feisty people and seems happy to engage in repartee with them. The Syro-Phoenician woman (Mark 7:24–30) and blind Bartimaeus (Luke 18:35) come to mind. To the woman's surprised question, "How can you [a Jew] ask me [a Samaritan] for a drink?" (4:9), Jesus replies in the same vein, with wit, using the symbol of water to whet her inquisitive mind further by saying, "If you knew the gift of God and who it is that asks you for a drink, you would have asked him and he would have given you living water" (4:10). This reply, pregnant with concealed meaning, begs other questions: "So who are you?", "What is this gift of God?" and "What is this living water?" The woman responds ironically: "You have nothing to draw with and the well is deep. Where can you get this living water?" She then creates greater irony by saying, "Are you greater than our father Jacob?"

This last question leads into one of the great sayings and promises of the Gospel: "Everyone who drinks this water will be thirsty again, but whoever drinks the water I give them will never thirst. Indeed, the water I give them will become in them a spring of water welling up to eternal life" (4:13–14). It is an extraordinary promise, underlined later in Jesus's words on the last day of the Feast of Tabernacles (7:37–38). In response to this seemingly fantastic offer, the woman, who can recognize a good thing even if she has not fully understood it, says, "Sir, give me this water so that I won't get thirsty and have to keep coming here to draw water" (4:15). All seems to be going smoothly until Jesus says, "Go, call your husband and come back" (4:16). At this point, Jesus makes receiving his gracious promise contingent on the woman recognizing the truth about her life, about true worship, and about who he really is. Each of these issues will come out in the remaining part of the conversation.

Truth intervenes (4:17–26)

There is no doubt that the remaining part of the conversation takes on a slightly different tone, becoming serious and real, personal and universal, revelatory and eternal. To Jesus's probing command, "Call your husband", the woman gives a true, although only half-true, answer: "I have no husband." It is not, in the phrase of the court room, "the truth, the whole truth and nothing but the truth." So Jesus fills in the picture, saying, "You are right when you say you have no husband. The fact is you have had five husbands, and the man you now have is not your husband. What you have said is quite true" (4:18). Jesus's reply does not on the face of it appear condemnatory. It is not designed to induce guilt. It is more a recognition of the woman's weakness and the unstable and ropey quality of her life. But it shows two things about Jesus: his willingness to make us face the truth, however uncomfortable, as a prelude to our own healing, and his divine insight into the reality of our lives, which has always been part of the character of God (see Psalm 139:1–4).

What we notice in this Gospel is John's emphasis on truth. Indeed, the word truth (*alētheia*) occurs 25 times in John's Gospel compared to once in Matthew and three times in Mark and Luke.[39] Thus we are told at the outset, Jesus is "full of grace and truth" (1:14,17), and this statement is so important that it appears twice in the Prologue. Other important occurrences in the Gospel are implicit in the conversation with the Samaritan woman; in the statement "the truth will set you free" (8:32); in the "I am" sayings of Jesus, such as, "I am the way and the truth and the life" (14:6); in Jesus's prayer for his disciples in which he prays, "Sanctify them by the truth; your word is truth" (17:17); and in the conversation with Pilate in Jesus's trial, in which Pilate asks, "What is truth?" (18:38). Truth is thus a major theme of the Gospel. There are many types of truth: mathematical and scientific truth, historical truth, truth about current affairs, which is often suppressed in dictatorships, and spiritual truth. Truth in John's Gospel means reality: reality about God and who he is; reality about humankind and what we are like; and reality about God's work in the world and our response. In the course of this conversation, three truths appear. Firstly, the reality about the woman's life, her five husbands and her present partner; the reality about worship; and lastly, the reality about the identity of Jesus. Each is revealed.

The Samaritan woman recognizes that Jesus is at least a prophet (4:19), and thankful for an excuse to change the conversation away from her personal life, she asks a thorny question: "Our fathers worshipped on this mountain, but you Jews claim that the place where we must worship is in Jerusalem" (4:20). Far from treating the question as a diversionary tactic, Jesus reveals another universal and eternal truth. In one of the most profound statements about worship in the Bible we are told what it is:

> Believe me woman, a time is coming when you will worship the Father neither on this mountain [Mount Gerizim, where Samaritans worshipped] nor in Jerusalem. You Samaritans worship what you do not know; we worship what we do know,

---

39 Morris, *Gospel According to St John*, p. 294.

for salvation is from the Jews. Yet a time is coming and has now come when true worshippers will worship the Father in spirit and truth, for they are the kind of worshippers the Father seeks. God is spirit, and his worshippers must worship in spirit and in truth.

John 4:21–24

Jesus is laying down profound and eternal principles about worship which root our response to the reality, presence, holiness and love of God. We are called to worship, that is, to give expression to what he is due, both with praise and adoration, but also with the sacrifice of our lives (Romans 12:1). Yet worship must be marked by two fundamental principles, which are that it is done according to the truth and in the spirit. Once again, *truth* is to the fore. Samaritans could not fully worship according to the truth because they rejected much of the Old Testament, although now, of course, they had fresh opportunity to put that right by being taught and led by the Messiah. Then secondly, our worship must be according to the spirit, and although we might want to say that the Holy Spirit is implicitly meant here, in fact the meaning *here* of the same word (*pneuma*) is the human spirit, meaning the deepest places of our personalities. Thus, our worship is not a matter of invention, form, habit or tradition, but rather is according to the truth offered from deep within our human spirit. In other words, it is *real*, according to our thoughts, feelings and desires. William Temple (1881–1944), the short-lived Archbishop of Canterbury, put it well in his commentary on John's Gospel:

> Worship is the submission of all our nature to God. It is the quickening of conscience by his holiness; the nourishment of mind with his truth; the purifying of imagination by his beauty; the opening of the heart to his love; the surrender of will to his purpose—and all of this gathered up in adoration, the most selfless emotion of which our nature is capable and therefore the chief remedy for that self-centredness which is our original sin and the source of all sin. Yes—worship in spirit and truth is the way to the solution of perplexity and to liberation from sin.[40]

---

[40] William Temple, *Readings in St John's Gospel* (London: Macmillan, 1949), p. 68.

The reason for worship in spirit and truth is that God himself is the embodiment of truth (i.e., the final and original reality) and the Father to whom all worship is directed through the Son and in the Spirit is also himself spirit (4:24, *proskuneō*, Greek for "worship", means to do obeisance or prostrate oneself).[41] Once again what is said here bears out the truth and theological phrasing of the Prologue, in which John tells us, "No one has ever *seen* God [for he is not material], but God the One and Only [Jesus] who is at the Father's side, has made him known" (1:18).

Having received this answer to her rather diversionary question about worship, directing attention away from the uncomfortable revelation and truth about her own life, the woman shows her understanding of Messianic expectation, which, interestingly, is common even amongst Samaritans. She says, "I know that the Messiah is coming, [John adds] he who is called Christ; when he comes, he will show us all things" (4:25). Here is the height of irony in the conversation. For she has expressed her faith in the teaching and truth of the coming Messiah, which even as a Samaritan she holds to, while irony of ironies, the person of whom she speaks is here talking to her! Jesus responds by quietly saying in simple, dignified terms, "I who speak to you am he!" (4:26). Hidden in his reply is the divine name itself, "I am who I am" (see Exodus 3:14 and John 8:58). Indeed, the Greek in Jesus's reply to the woman reads: "I am, the one speaking to you." It is the only admission by Jesus of his Messianic status before his trial in front of the High Priest and Pilate (Matthew 26:64; John 18:37), and typically it is made to a non-Jew, a despised Samaritan, and a woman whose name we don't know, and who has been in six relationships with men! And at that moment the disciples return from their shopping trip (4:27).

Response of the disciples and the Samaritans (4:27–42)

In many ways, this entire narrative, known by theologians as the Second Discourse (the first being the conversation with Nicodemus along with John's editorial comment), reads like a play in three acts: Jesus's initial

---

41 Walter Bauer, William Arndt and F. Wilbur Gingrich, *Greek Lexicon* (Chicago: University of Chicago Press, 1957), p. 723.

tiredness and the disciples' departure; the central second act being the conversation with the woman; and the third act beginning with the return of the disciples (Scene I) and then the response of the Samaritans (Scene II). We have reached the third act, in which the disciples and the Samaritans have contrasting reactions.

The Samaritans could not be more exemplary in their response, unlike the Jewish response in Chorazin, Bethsaida and Capernaum (see Matthew 11:20–24). Despite all the teaching and miracles in those villages, they do not respond with faith. Yet these Samaritan villages near Sychar (Shechem?) are welcoming and believing. The evangelist is the woman at the well, who is still a little uncertain about Jesus's exact identity. But so excited is she that she leaves her water jar, the very reason for being there, and makes haste back to her village. "Come, [an important Johannine word, see 1:39; 1:46] see a man who told me everything I ever did. Could this be the Christ [Messiah]?" So excited and impressed with Jesus is she that she expresses her astonishment with hyperbole: he told me everything I *ever* did. She then tentatively suggests that he might be the Christ: "It is as though a negative answer might be expected, but a positive one is hoped for."[42] Her testimony sparks interest in a sleepy village, where probably little of note happens, and several villagers go out to meet Jesus themselves. They ask him to stay with them (4:40), which he does for two days. Many initially believe because of the woman's testimony, but many more come to believe because of their direct contact and conversation with Jesus (4:41–42). Indeed, the testimony of the villagers becomes emphatic: "We know that this man really is the Saviour of the world" (4:42b). The Samaritans are extraordinary in their believing response, and neither is it an incident that John the Apostle was likely to forget. Indeed, early on in the narrative of Acts, it is Peter and John who go to Samaria, following the evangelistic mission of Philip the Evangelist, one of the Seven (Acts 6:5,6), and they pray for the Samaritan believers to receive the Holy Spirit (Acts 8:14–17). Is it fanciful to think that some of them might have been the Samaritans who met Jesus when he stayed in their village?

---

42   Morris, *Gospel According to St John*, p. 275.

The response of the disciples is more muted than that of the woman. They are nonplussed. When the disciples return from their foraging, they are "surprised" (Greek *thaumázō*, more literally "astonished") that he is speaking with a woman, let alone a Samaritan woman of dubious reputation (4:27). Despite their astonishment they do not pluck up courage to ask, "Why are you talking to her?" Quite clearly in their minds, Jesus breaking convention in this way borders on the scandalous. What they do is urge Jesus to eat something, knowing he was hungry before their departure, but he appears to be satisfied. Indeed, he goes as far as to say, "I have food to eat that you know nothing about" (4:32). This only serves to increase their confusion. They think he has been given some food (4:33). But Jesus explains that there is another type of food that sustains him, which "is to do the will of him who sent me and to finish his work" (4:34). Here is another insight into the Father/Son relationship so prevalent in this Gospel, underlining the unity of purpose in the Trinity. Doing the work of the Father and completing it is a kind of food for the Son. Not only this, but Jesus goes on to say there is an urgency about this work. The harvest is virtually ready (4:35b). Just as in agriculture there must be sowers and reapers, so in this spiritual harvest there will be those who sow and those who reap. In the case of the disciples, John the Baptist and others have prepared the ground and sown the seed; now it is their privilege to harvest the spiritual fruit. In the very next verses, the believing Samaritans are certainly evidence of the fruit.

The conversation with the Samaritan woman is immensely fruitful. It demonstrates the versatility and extent of Jesus's ministry, which proceeds on the lines of grace and truth to Jew and non-Jew alike. In these opening chapters, Jesus has collected a community of disciples around him, and has been identified as the Lamb of God and the bringer of the Spirit. Furthermore, his reach extends from the elite and the aristocratic, such as Nicodemus, who is told plainly that he must be born again, to an isolated woman with a waterpot, shielding the truth of her sixth partner and meeting a man who tells her "everything I ever did" (4:39b). In time, both Nicodemus (19:39) and the woman bear the badge of belonging; they *believe* and in believing they have life (1:4).

CHAPTER 6

Two Signs and a Discourse

John 4:43–5:47

The plan of the Gospel continues, interweaving signs with discourses, and here we have two more signs (the second and the third), and a third discourse (after the one with Nicodemus and another with the woman at the well).

Jesus moves north to Galilee from Shechem (or Sychar) in Samaria, about 35 miles away. Although Jesus has warned his disciples that a prophet rarely receives honour in his home territory (4:44), they are in fact warmly welcomed by the Galileans. Many have seen Jesus in Jerusalem and have heard of his impact during the Feast of Passover (4:45). Once again Jesus goes to Cana, about 15 miles west of Galilee in the hill country north of the fashionable town of Sepphoris, which had been rebuilt by Herod Antipas, and of Nazareth, his hometown. There Jesus meets a royal official whose son is seriously ill in Capernaum. This official or courtier probably served the family of Herod the Tetrarch and thus represents a third type of person after the elite religious leader, Nicodemus, and the lowly unnamed Samaritan woman. Once again, the boundless ministry of Jesus is on display. The official is desperate that Jesus heal his son, and begs him to come down with him to Capernaum. Having chided the people that they require miracles to believe, Jesus promises that this man's son will live (4:48–50). The official, whose name we also do not know, takes Jesus "at his word" and returns to Capernaum, meeting his servants en route, who tell him that his son is better. Further enquiry shows that his son recovered at the seventh hour (the perfect moment) and the very hour when Jesus promised he would recover.

Hearing this, both the official and his household "believe". It is another classic case of healing leading to belief.

The next sign, which follows immediately, occurs in Jerusalem at one of the feasts of the Jews (5:1). This healing is more contentious because it takes place on the Sabbath, which leads to a heated argument with the Jewish leaders about the identity of Jesus, which in turn forms the background to the next discourse (5:16–47). It takes place at a healing centre called the Pool of Bethesda, which was surrounded by five covered colonnades and was on the north side of the Temple Mount near the Sheep Gate (5:2).

The Pool of Bethesda had become a hospital for the sick. We are told that over time a multitude (Greek: *plēthos*, from which we get the word "plethora") of sick people gathered there in hope of a cure. A tradition had grown up that from time to time an angel stirred the water, and the first person to be immersed following this would be cured (this is explained in John 5:3b–4 following some ancient manuscript authorities). While visiting the pool, Jesus runs into a man who has apparently been there for 38 years. Jesus asks him if he wants to get well, and hearing that he does in so many words (see 5:7) commands him to pick up his mat and walk healed from the pool. The man follows Jesus's instruction and amazingly finds that he can both walk and pick up the mat on which he has been lying. But there are two points which are germane to the healing: it takes place on the Sabbath and the man does not know who it is that has "made him well" (5:11).

The ever watchful and present religious leaders see the healed man carrying his mat, which to them is an offence for it constitutes work on the Sabbath. This is one of many incidents in the Gospels of Jesus healing on the Sabbath. Indeed, a very similar incident occurs just a few chapters later in the healing of the man born blind (see John 9:14). This is part of a long-running dispute with the Pharisees and Scribes about the observance of the Sabbath laws in which Jesus maintains that doing good on the Sabbath, such as healing, whatever it involves, is permitted, for "the Sabbath was made for man not man for the Sabbath" (Mark 2:27).

Only later does the man who was healed discover the identity of the person who has healed him with a word. Interestingly, Jesus finds him in the Temple area (5:14) and gives him a severe warning that he should desist from sin, whatever that might be, so that nothing worse happens to him. Here the man's condition seems connected to some volitional sin, although in the case of the blind man whom Jesus heals on the Sabbath in John 9 there is no such connection (see 9:3). Despite the warning and his healing, the man ungratefully betrays Jesus to the rulers, telling them who it is that has healed him (5:15).

This healing, which is the third sign of the Gospel, takes place during one of the feasts of the Jews (5:1), quite possibly Pentecost or Shavout—also called the Feast of Weeks, celebrating the Wheat Harvest—which falls between Passover (4:45) and the Feast of Tabernacles (7:2). Once again, Jerusalem would have been filled with visitors or pilgrims from across the Diaspora, and it was in this atmosphere that the leaders of the Jews sought to persecute him (Greek, *diōkō*, meaning "to persecute" or "drive out"). As one translation of this verse put it, "It was works of this kind done on the Sabbath that stirred the Jews to persecute Jesus" (NEB). These events form the background to the discourse or argument that follows. At the heart of this debate is the claim of Jesus that the Father is working even on the Sabbath, and that as his Son (inferred from 5:17 where he calls God "my Father"), he is likewise working. In a single sentence Jesus has radically expanded the scope for offence.

My Father and I (5:16–30)

In the space of the next few sentences, Jesus lays bare the unique relationship of Father and Son in a way that does not exist elsewhere in Scripture. It could not therefore be more significant. It is important to understand that Jesus's description of the respective roles of Father and Son is an answer to the indictment of the Jews that he is breaking the Sabbath and, furthermore, that he is blaspheming by "even calling God his own Father, making himself equal with God" (5:18). Of course, this is precisely what Jesus was doing, and now, in his answer to the Jews, i.e., their leaders, Jesus explains the relationship of the Father and the Son and the honour in which the Son is held by the Father. What we find in these verses is a general reality of reciprocity and mutuality between Father and Son. Indeed, the term "son" (Greek: *ó uiós*) is used eight times in these verses (19–26) and only five times in the rest of the Gospel, thereby underlining the importance of this passage in describing the status and role of the Son.

Here Jesus makes a number of ground-breaking claims to do with his actions and their origin: his power to give life and his right to judge. In each of these spheres of activity, Jesus operates or works with the Father. First, concerning his actions, Jesus says his miracles and the shape of his ministry follow a pattern laid down by his Father, although he expresses this in more dynamic terms. He says: he can do nothing *by himself*. In other words, he is not an independent operator. Jesus gives us the maxim that he "can only do what he sees his Father doing, because whatever the Father does the Son also does" (5:19). It is "through a continual and uninterrupted communion between Father and Son" that Jesus knows what he is to do.[43] So, for instance, it must have been because of such understanding that Jesus does not go to the sick Lazarus immediately (see 11:4–6) but waits until he dies, so that he might raise him from death. Such confidence must surely have come from a contemplation of the Father's will in that and every other situation. Likewise, disciples today might wait to discern the Father's will and pursue that, rather than undertaking human programmes, which are good but unbidden. Nor does the Father hide his will from the Son, because he loves him and shows him all he does (5:20).

Secondly, Jesus is a life-giver and has been charged by the Father to give life wherever. There are few more powerful illustrations of this than a fresco in a chapel called Chora built in the tenth century in Constantinople, present-day Istanbul. Here Jesus is depicted taking hold of the hands of Adam and Eve, who are dead in their graves, and pulling them from death into new life with great energy. Jesus is thus dynamically presented as the life-giver. "For just as the Father raises the dead and gives them life, even so the Son gives life to whom he is pleased to give it" (5:21). Or again Jesus says, "I tell you the truth, a time is coming and has now come when the dead will hear the voice of the Son of God and those who hear will live. For as the Father has life in himself, so he has

---

43   Morris, *Gospel According to St John*, p. 312.

granted the Son to have life in himself" (5:25–26). From the beginning Jesus is a life-giver, and nor is there ever a time when he is not.

Thirdly, and this theme runs through these verses like a purple thread, Jesus is the Judge. The Father has entrusted all judgement to the Son, so that the Son may be truly honoured (5:23). Judgement will be on the basis of faith, showing itself in works (see Matthew 25:14–30 and 31–46). Here Jesus puts it like this, "Those who have done good will rise to live, and those who have done evil will rise to be condemned" (5:29). As we look out on a world riven by war, injustice, harsh treatment, abuse and exploitation, we are reminded that there will be a reckoning. It may be hard to find culprits and bring them to justice in this life, but there remains a final assize. This judgement provides the muscle to the second commandment—the one that encapsulates all other commandments relating to people—in which we are called to "love your neighbour as yourself" (Matthew 22:39).

In these verses, which are so critical to understanding the relationship between the Father and Son, Jesus draws back the veil on their bond. As we know from the Prologue, it is an eternal relationship (see 1:1), in which Father and Son share the same substance (*ousia*), as fourth-century theologians like Athanasius, the Cappadocians and Ambrose put it. The bond that ties them together and enables this mutual sharing is love (see 5:20). But the word for love here is not the *agape* (selfless love) of John 3:16, in which God so loves the world that he gives his Son, but rather the *philia* love of friendship. The eternal friendship between Father and Son is the bond in which life, judgement and mutual honour are shared. It is a friendship into which disciples are to be drawn by the influence of the Spirit, as we shall later see.

The role of testimony

The last part of John 5, and this Third Discourse of the Gospel, deals with the identity of the Son and the role of testimony, which is a particularly Jewish notion. There appear to be seven witnesses in the Gospel: the Father, the words and works of Jesus, Jesus himself, the Spirit, Moses and the Scriptures he wrote, and John the Baptist. In addition, there are human witnesses who come forward in the Gospel narrative, such as the woman at the well. Here Jesus brings forward several of these witnesses (*marturía*) who give testimony of his true identity. Once again, the search is on for true or valid testimony which would stand up in a court of law. Jesus firstly refers obliquely to the Father, "who testifies in my favour" (5:32). He then refers to John the Baptist but says that human witness is inferior to that of Father, Son and Spirit (5:36a). The witness that Jesus refers to next is the work he has been given by the Father (5:36b), the Father whose form (Greek: *eidos*, meaning "outward appearance") or voice the Jews have not seen or heard (5:37).[44] The last witness is the Scriptures. Despite having diligently studied them, the Jews have not come to Jesus, their chief subject, to receive life. This would be like a person going into a restaurant and studying the menu extensively, but never ordering any of the dishes and instead eating the menu! The Scriptures speak supremely of Christ, but to benefit from them a person must receive him and have life. Many of the Jews refused to come to him.

The point that Jesus is making here is that there is plenty of evidence, testimony and witnesses, but the Jews refuse to pay attention to it. One of the chief reasons for this is that the Jews loved to receive praise from one another (5:41–44). This craving for praise effectively blocks the search for praise from God. Unlike them, Jesus does not look for or accept praise from people (5:41). His sole concern is to please the Father and be praised by him.

The final twist in this discourse is that the very person they pride themselves on knowing and studying, namely Moses, will finally stand as their accuser. Because they have mistaken the menu for the food and the signpost for the destination, they are unable to receive life. They search the Scriptures, but will not come to the person about whom these chiefly speak to receive life by believing. Their problem is truly believing and here we come to one of the central words of the Gospel, first used in the Prologue (see 1:12) where those with a new birth are those "who believed in his name". Believing is what people are called to do, and in believing there is life. The verb "believing" (*pisteúō*) is found 98 times in the Gospel, although the word "faith" (*pístis*) is completely absent.

---

44   Bauer, Arndt and Gingrich, *Greek Lexicon*, p. 276.

Perhaps the reason for this is John's desire to stress the *activity of faith.* Belief is not so much a single event or a settled existence as *an ongoing dynamic of trust* in the person of Christ. This is true believing. And if they can't believe Moses, how are they going to believe Jesus of whom he spoke?

CHAPTER 7

The Bread of Life

John 6:1–71

In many ways, John 6 has the Gospel in a chapter. In it we have two more signs: the fourth and the fifth—the Feeding of the Five Thousand and the Walking on the Water. There is also a long discourse: the fourth, centred on one of the great "I am" sayings of the Gospel: "I am the Bread of Life" (6:35). And finally, there is the confession of Peter (6:67–71). It is also the last piece of recorded ministry in Galilee before the narrative shifts to Jerusalem and its surrounding area.

Jesus now travels to a remote part of Palestine. He goes to the far (eastern) shore of Galilee or the Sea of Tiberias, which then took its name from the Emperor Tiberias (AD 14–37) who had succeeded Augustus (27 BC–14 AD). Tiberias was the stepson of Augustus, and son of the Empress Livia by a former marriage. He succeeded as emperor when Gaius and Lucius Caesar, Augustus' two grandsons by his only child Julia, died prematurely. Tiberias was emperor for most of Jesus's adult life and gave his name to a new town on the western shore of Galilee which became the region's principal city. Jesus crossed over to the east, but was followed by a huge crowd which later we are told numbered 5,000 men. They followed him because "they saw the miraculous signs he had performed on the sick" (6:2). On the far side Jesus walked up a mountainside, sat down with his disciples, and began to teach.

Always conscious of the Jewish calendar, John tells us that it was close to the Jewish Passover. If that is the case then it is the second Passover of the Gospel narrative, the first being recorded in Jerusalem (see 2:13,23). The Feast of Passover is the necessary context for the principal sign of this chapter, the Feeding of the Five Thousand, recalling the feeding of Israel in the desert with manna and the liberation of Israel in the Exodus. Now one greater than Moses is among them both *to nourish* and *to liberate* all who come to him and believe. It is this background of Roman occupation signalled by the re-naming of the lake and the principal town of the region, and of Jewish expectation signalled by the Jewish feast of Passover which recalls the Israelite liberation from Egypt, that provides the backdrop to the events and teaching of this chapter.

The Feeding of the Five Thousand

Apart from the resurrection, the Feeding of the Five Thousand is the only miracle to be recorded in all four Gospels. We might ask ourselves why this is. The answer could be that it looks back to the great feeding of the Jewish people in the wilderness (Exodus 16) and demonstrates that in the power of Christ "all our hungers are satisfied". It also demonstrates that Jesus is able to provide for our needs and fulfil his purposes from whatever he is given.

At the outset of the account, Jesus deliberately challenges Philip, who comes from nearby Bethsaida in the north-east corner of Galilee, about what to do. Often the go-to man among the disciples (see also 1:43ff., 12:21 and 14:8), Philip sees the impossibility of the situation, rather than a solution. "Eight months' wages would not buy enough bread for each one to have a bite!" (6:7) he replies, and that is if the shops are open and fully stocked! Andrew comes up with a more promising suggestion. There is a boy in the crowd from a modest background who has five small barley loaves and two fish. He famously adds, "but how far will they go among so many?" (6:9). The miracle or sign proceeds from the small boy *giving up* his packed lunch to Jesus and a remarkable miracle taking place as a result.

The focus in John's account, however, is not so much on the miracle or sign itself, indicating the authority of Jesus over creation, as on more symbolic lessons. These amount to the sacred hospitality enshrined in the sign, the care for food and the underlying message of the sign about which Jesus teaches extensively.

The idea of *sacred hospitality* is shown in the sign itself, which also anticipates the Eucharist, something Jesus explains later (see 6:51b,53–59). John appears to have conflated this teaching about the Eucharist with the sign itself. In the first instance, and in preparation for the sign, Jesus brings some order to the vast crowd, which is estimated at 5,000 men (6:10), with presumably women and children besides, by getting them to sit down in organized groups (see Mark 6:39). They are invited to recline, and to be at ease (Greek: *ānapiptō*). The place itself is hospitable, having "much grass" (6:10a), and is not, therefore, a scree-filled hillside. When they are seated Jesus acts as the host and prayerfully gives thanks. (The Greek word is *eùcharistéō*, from which we get eucharist, whereas the Synoptic Gospel writers use *eùlogeō* instead, meaning simply praise. The use of *eùcharistéō* may indicate a more technical use of the idea of giving thanks, which had by now taken its place in the early Church, with its links to the Lord's Supper.) Having given thanks and broken the loaves and fish, Jesus distributes them to the crowd through the disciples. Presumably the miracle happens in the disciples' hands, and they give away as much as the people want (6:11b). When the crowd has had enough, or literally "is filled", Jesus commands that the fragments or leftovers be gathered up, presumably meaning the pieces of bread and fish scattered around the hillside which have not been eaten.

Jesus shows his respect for the *preciousness of food* by commanding that these leftovers be picked up. The words of Jesus that ring out are, "let nothing be wasted" (6:12b). To the shame of our modern society, we throw away far too much food. It is estimated that as much as a quarter of food purchased is thrown away. Although composting is now common in households and local councils, disposing of surplus food still leads to great wastage. Sales pitches in supermarkets often lead to people over-buying and lack of handy recipes means that "finishing up" food is neglected. Added to this, sell-by dates can lead to failure to use foods that have hardly deteriorated. The signs are that, having made progress towards millennium goals in the earlier part of the century, climate change, desertification, flooding and now war in the breadbasket of Ukraine and Russia threaten global food security. Rocketing prices of essential foodstuffs such as wheat, barley and cooking oils are causing social unrest. According to the IMF, "record-high food prices could have implications for social unrest in some emerging and frontier markets."[45]

But on the hillside of north-east Galilee, the result of a gathering up of leftovers is that 12 small wicker baskets are filled.[46] In the febrile atmosphere of Jewish independence and Messianic expectation, the result of this miracle is initially political. Jesus knows that, not content to acclaim him a prophet or the expected Prophet (see also 1:21 and Deuteronomy 18:14ff.), many in the crowd want to make him a king in the mould of their own Messianic expectations, with the purpose of marching against the Romans. But as the Jewish rebellion of AD 70 shows, this would prove a futile objective. Knowing this to be their intent, Jesus slips out of the crowd and finds a deserted and hidden spot in the hills. Meanwhile, and after dark, the disciples embark for the other side of the lake, aiming to reach Capernaum on the north-west side. They cross the shorter part of the lake, but it proves hard going.

Following the Feeding of the Five Thousand and the gradual dispersal of the crowd, Jesus has retired to the hills alone while the disciples leave by boat after dark (6:17). It is at this point that Jesus decides to re-join the disciples by walking to them across the water. Meanwhile, they are struggling to make progress against "a great wind". Unlike the Synoptic Gospels, there is little description of the disciples' reaction to Jesus's approach across the water and nor is there mention of Peter trying to reach Jesus by himself walking across the water (see Matthew 14:22ff.) to meet him. All we are told is that the disciples are terrified when they see Jesus walking on the water towards them. In John's account, Jesus announces his identity with the redolent phrase which translates literally as "I am" (Greek: *Egō eìmi*), but is generally rendered "It is me!" The account then ends somewhat mysteriously with the boat immediately and inexplicably reaching the shore, and the wind completely abating (see also Mark 6:50–52).

The crowds are mystified by Jesus's travel arrangements. Some realize that the disciples have left in the only boat without Jesus, raising the question of his own transport across the lake. A further crowd seems to

---

[45]   Mehreen Khan, "Inflation Surge", *The Times*, 20 April 2022, p. 34.

[46]   Morris, *Gospel According to St John*, p. 354.

have come across from Tiberias a day late and, finding neither Jesus nor the disciples, likewise embark for Capernaum (6:24). When the crowd finds Jesus, the fourth discourse of the Gospel begins.

The fourth discourse on the Bread of Life (6:25–59)

This discourse divides into three parts. The first part goes to verse 42, the second from verse 43 to 52, and the third from 53–59. The three parts are marked by increasing hostility towards Jesus on account of his claims. The discourse takes place in Capernaum, where the crowd have followed Jesus from the other side of the lake. Jesus senses that the only reason that they have turned up is because they "ate the loaves" and had their fill, which is probably true. They are literally looking for another free and satisfying meal. Jesus gently rebukes them, advising them, "Do not work for the food that spoils, but for food that endures to eternal life, which the Son of Man will give you", because "on him God the Father has placed his seal of approval" (6:27). Sensitive to his correction, they now rightly ask a critical question, "What must we do to do the works God requires?" (6:28). In keeping with the rest of the Gospel, Jesus replies, "The work of God is this: *to believe* in the one he has sent" (6:29). However, the Jewish crowd, in keeping with their own general mentality, demand further signs in order to believe! (See 1 Corinthians 1:22 where Paul writes, "Jews demand miraculous signs and Greeks look for wisdom.") It is ironic, however, that they should give way to this instinctive desire for signs, for many in the crowd have already manifestly benefitted from one in the Feeding of the Five Thousand, and many have also realized that Jesus crossed the lake by another miraculous sign (see 6:22). The demand for a sign is then pushed further by the crowd, who want Jesus to do what "Moses did for Israel in the desert", ignoring the fact that the bread that was supplied in the desert came from the Father, and not from Moses.

As with the woman at the well and the symbol of water, Jesus is more than happy to take up the metaphor of bread and declare, "I tell you the truth, it is not Moses who has given you the bread from heaven ... For the bread of God is he who comes down from heaven and gives life to the world" (6:32,33). Not surprisingly, hearing of such a free offer, the crowd says, "From now on give us this bread" (compare with the Samaritan woman's saying in 4:15). Having brought the crowd to this point, Jesus makes his own emphatic declaration in the form of one of the great "I am" sayings: "I am the bread of life. He who comes to me will never go hungry, and he who believes in me will never be thirsty" (6:35).

Jesus now confronts an inconvenient truth, namely that it is possible to see the most remarkable signs and still not believe (6:36). Believing is not automatic. Indeed, Jesus himself concludes his parable of Dives and Lazarus by saying as much (see Luke 16:31). Given that this is possible—i.e., seeing and not believing—Jesus looks behind the process of believing and suggests there is a double action at work in belief: on the one hand a person must believe, but on the other the Father must also draw that person to faith. Or, to use different language, the Father must give that person as a gift to the Son. In such a context, it is the Son's purpose not to lose any who are thus given. (For elaboration of this thinking, read Jesus's High Priestly Prayer, so called, in which he further speaks of, and prays about, this charge. See 17:6–8,12.)

Jesus concludes this section of the discourse with statements about his own earthly task: to "lose none of all that he [the Father] has given me, but raise them up on the last day" (6:39). Jesus thus combines the teaching given in Chapter 5 that the Father has granted him power to summon the dead from the grave (see 5:28) with the responsibility of losing none who are given him, besides Judas.

Jesus finishes with a majestic saying that stands as a further summary of the Gospel: "For my Father's will is that everyone who looks to the Son and believes in him shall have eternal life, and I will raise them up at the last day" (6:40). Nevertheless, Jesus proves his own point that it is possible to see and hear, and not believe (see also the Prologue 1:10–11). For although the crowd have witnessed a sign or miracle, and indeed have personally benefitted by filling their stomachs, and although they have heard his teaching, some of them nevertheless grumble about him saying that he is the bread of life come down from heaven. They complain because they knew him as the kid from down the road—the son of Joseph, "whose father and mother we know"—so "how can he now say, 'I came down from heaven'?" (6:42). In other words, they take offence at him; but it is about to get a lot worse.

Jesus now reiterates and elaborates what he has previously said in the earlier section (6:25–42), but he begins this new section (6:43–51) by rebuking them for their grumbling (6:43). Grumbling was part of the experience of the Exodus, for which the Israelites were rebuked, but it seems not much has changed (Exodus 16:2; Numbers 11:4–6; 21:4,5). Once again Jesus emphasizes that believing is not a matter of one's own will. It is a gift (see Ephesians 2:8) or, as the Prologue puts it, Christians are "born not of natural descent, nor of human decision or a husband's will, but born of God" (1:13). It is the Father who gives believers to the Son or who draws them into faith by his own operation. Jesus affirms this further by quoting from Isaiah that all God's people are both drawn and taught by God himself (6:45). Those who listen to the Father also come to the Son: there is no distinction and no division between them. Indeed, only the Son has seen the Father—not materially, for God is Spirit, but spiritually. Spiritually, the Son has truly beheld the Father. (Again, see the Prologue 1:18: "No one has ever seen God, but God the One and Only who is at the Father's side, has made him known.")

Jesus now goes on to make further claims of the bread that comes down from heaven (6:48). Believing in this bread grants eternal or everlasting life (same Greek word: *aiōnios*). The distinction between the manna in the wilderness wanderings and the bread that Jesus gives is that Christ-as-bread confers eternal life (6:50). Eating this bread means a person will not spiritually die, but will live into the new eternal age (6:51; Greek: *aiōn*, from which we derive *aeons*). Jesus then radically changes the metaphor, saying the life-giving principle is not bread but his own flesh, which he will give for the "life of the world". This refers to his sacrificial death, already indicated by John the Baptist's cry, "Look, the Lamb of God who takes away the sin of the world" (1:29). It is this transposition of the word "bread" into "flesh", striking and arresting as it is, that creates further opportunity for offence in the crowd. The giving of flesh for the life of the world is a memorable statement—shocking, crude even—[47]and it gets a strong reaction from some of the crowd, who say, "How can this man give us his flesh to eat?" (6:52). Jesus's response to this objection is the substance of the final and third part of the discourse.

---

[47]   Morris, *Gospel According to St John*, p. 374.

Jesus elaborates on his initial saying that his flesh is to be given "for the life of the world" by saying, "unless you eat the flesh of the Son of Man and drink his blood you have no life in you" (6:53). This is deliberately shocking and deeply thought-provoking. He then says positively of any believer who does these things, i.e., eats his flesh and drinks his blood, "I will raise them up at the last day" (6:54). For his flesh and blood is real food (6:55).

Again, *real* is synonymous with the Greek word for *truth*—i.e., it is true food. The outcome of this eating and drinking is that the believer remains or abides in Christ, in the same way that the Father sent and resides in the Son and vice versa (6:57). These are strong Johannine themes: the believer is called to remain; the remaining is mutual and reciprocal. As the believer remains in Christ, so Christ remains in the believer; as the Son remains in the Father, so the Father remains in the Son. The outcome of this spiritual eating of the bread is that Christ lives in the believer.

But what does it mean to eat Christ's flesh and drink his blood? It would seem there are two levels of meaning. First and foremost, it means participating in the death of Christ by faith. Given that by c.AD 90, when this Gospel was quite possibly written and the worship of the Church now familiarly included the Eucharist, it would not seem remarkable if Jesus's words not only meant believing in his sacrificial death, but also partaking with faith in the Last Supper that seals by a sign the benefits of that death upon a believer. Indeed, Justin Martyr wrote this of the centrality of the Eucharist in Rome in his *First Apology* of c.AD 155:

> And this food is called the EùXaristía—the Eucharist—of which no one is allowed to partake but the man who believes that the things which we teach are true, and who has been washed with the washing that is for the remission of sins, and unto regeneration, and who is so living as Christ enjoined. For not as common bread and common drink do we receive these; but in like manner as Jesus Christ our Saviour, having been made flesh by the Word of God, hath both flesh and blood for our salvation, so likewise have we been taught that the food which is blessed by the prayer of his word, and from which our blood and flesh by

transmutation are nourished, is the flesh and blood of that Jesus who was made flesh.[48]

Furthermore, no less a figure from the Reformation than John Calvin, writing in his great work *Institutes of the Christian Religion*, having made the point, as above, that participating in Christ's flesh and blood is primarily believing and partaking in his death by faith, goes on to say:

> That sacred communion of flesh and blood by which Christ infuses his life into us, just as if it penetrates our bones and marrow, he testifies and seals in the Supper. And that, not by presenting a vain and empty sign, but by them exerting an efficacy of the Spirit by which he fulfils what he promises.[49]

If this is the meaning of Jesus's words about eating his flesh and drinking his blood, it is not altogether surprising that the crowd misunderstood and found it a hard saying. After all, his disciples did not generally understand that his death, which would involve violence, the spilling of blood and the tearing of his flesh, still lay some way in the future. Not even his closest disciples understood its reality and significance yet: i.e., that it would be the means of salvation in which all must participate. On the basis of all the evidence of his life and ministry thus far, some followed, but others turned back. It is time to evaluate the response to Jesus at this critical juncture of his ministry before he turned resolutely to Jerusalem and his destiny there.

---

[48] Justin Martyr, *First Apology*, TANF, Vol. 1 (Grand Rapids, MI: Eerdmans, 1975), p. 185.

[49] John Calvin, *Institutes of Christian Religion*, Bk. IV, Ch. 17.10 (Edinburgh: T & T Clark, 1875), p. 563.

The response of the disciples (6:60–71)

Jesus is aware that his words have offended some, and that some of the more fair-weather disciples on the fringe of his followers think now to leave. Such is the fickleness of humankind that quite probably 24 hours previously some of these disciples had thought to make him their king (see 6:15), but as said earlier by John, Jesus knows what is in person and what changeable creatures we can be (see 2:25). Jesus implies that if they have been offended by his words, how much more offended might they be in the future to see the Son of Man crucified, risen and ascended to the Father. Jesus then reiterates a principle of his teaching already given to Nicodemus (see 3:5,6), that it is the Spirit that gives life and his own words, just spoken, are from the Spirit and are life-giving (see 6:63). Once again, we see the interweaving of Jesus and the Spirit. It is through their joint working that salvation comes.

But Jesus is aware that choices lie ahead for the disciples. Indeed, to follow is to choose and indeed to go on choosing, or we might say, to go on believing. Some of those with Jesus do not believe (see 6:64), and worse, some of them might betray him (6:64). And for there to be real faithfulness on the part of the disciple, there must not only be believing or faith, *but the work of the Father in drawing that person to faith.* If this is a mystery, it is nonetheless a vital part of conversion. We must appeal to a person to believe, but must pray at the same time that the Father draws him or her to the Son (6:65). In the space of a few verses, Jesus has shown how each member of the Godhead or Trinity is involved in creating true discipleship. For a lack of this mysterious activity of the Godhead and of true understanding on the part of these disciples many "turned back and no longer followed him" (6:66).

Having spoken more generally to these more peripheral disciples listening to him in Capernaum that day, Jesus turns his full attention to the Twelve. He asks them if they want to leave too. The answers are mixed. Peter, as is often the case, stands up and speaks for the Twelve (see Acts 2:14), or should I say the Eleven? His answer could not be more confident in its ringing endorsement both of Jesus as the "Holy One of God" and in its deep appreciation that only Jesus has "the words of eternal life" (6:68). Despite this ringing endorsement of him as the

Messiah, Jesus is not carried away. He knows that among his closest disciples there is a traitor or betrayer: Judas Iscariot. Presumably Judas makes a show of belief, but all the while is thinking, "what is in it for me?" Of all the Gospel writers, John identifies him as a thief who already regularly steals from the common purse (12:6). It is the thought of a further payment from the High Priests that drives him to betray Jesus (Matthew 26:14–16). Made vulnerable by his greed, Satan finds a ready entry point into Judas's life and entices him to betray (John 13:27). And in the context of this extended discourse in John 6 about believing, Judas neither sincerely believes and nor have the Father and Spirit drawn him to the Son. The interaction between personal responsibility and divine calling is played out in tragedy in Judas's life. And with this contrast between ringing endorsement and impending betrayal, John's narrative leaves Galilee for good and the story continues to unfold in Jerusalem.

CHAPTER 8

Among Divided Opinion:
A Universal Offer

John 7:1–52

As we read this chapter of the Gospel, we can almost feel the spiritual temperature rising. We have not yet reached the turning point (Chapter 12), but the levels of opposition against Jesus appear to be growing, and the uniqueness of his offer of life is becoming clearer. Each seems to grow with the other.

Another Jewish festival, the Feast of Tabernacles (Hebrew *sukkot*, meaning "tabernacles" or "tents"), has arrived. This is one of the great Jewish festivals which every male Israelite is required to attend (see Exodus 23:14–19; Leviticus 23:39–43). The Feast of Tabernacles celebrates the festival of ingathering or harvest, as well as the wilderness years of the Israelites in the desert. It is a time of joy, ending with the Simchat Torah, dancing, and giving thanks for the Law.

Discussion with Jesus's brothers
and in Jerusalem (7:1–13)

An element of secrecy now surrounds Jesus's movements, and he will not readily accept the suggestions of his brothers. They appear to advise him that if he wants to be accepted by the people as a religious leader, he must go to Jerusalem: "no one who wants to become a public figure acts in secret. Since you are doing these things, show yourself to the world" (7:4). We quickly see that his brothers, presumably of Mary and

Joseph, are struggling with three issues. Essentially, we are told that at this stage they do not believe in him, meaning they do not believe that he is the Messiah, or the Son of God (7:5). Being too familiar with him, and having grown up together, they cannot see past his humanity to appreciate his divinity. Furthermore, not content with the signs that he has performed in Galilee—such as feeding the five thousand, walking on water, and turning water into wine—they want to see more miracles in Judea. The problem with drawing attention to himself in Judea, however, is that Jesus has many enemies there among the religious hierarchy that dominates Jerusalem. As John indicates at the outset, "the Jews there were waiting to take his life" (7:1). In consequence, Jesus does not want to go up openly to the feast, in case he is either prematurely adopted by some nationalistic elements as a rebel leader against the Romans (see 6:15), or is quickly picked out for premature punishment by the Jews on account of his claim to be the Messiah. He has to play his hand carefully.

The determining factor behind the timing of Jesus's arrival in Jerusalem is ensuring that it does not evoke a premature hostile response. He tells his brothers, "the right time for me has not yet come" (7:6). The Greek word that Jesus uses here for "time" is *kairòs*, not *chronos*, which simply means the passing of sequential time, rather than an eventful or critical moment. Although the word "hour" is often used in the Gospel (see 2:4 and 12:27), this is the only instance where the word *kairòs* is used. Jesus clearly does not want to precipitate his arrest: there is more preparation of the disciples to complete, more deeds to perform, and more words from his Father to teach. Knowing the hostility of the Jews, because he has testified to the evil that is in people, Jesus goes secretly up to Jerusalem after the beginning of this seven-day feast, following his brothers who have gone up at the beginning (7:10).

Halfway through the festival (see 7:11 and 14) the Jews are looking out for him. By this time, there is a division among the people over the trustworthiness and sincerity of Jesus. Some say he is a good man, others that he is a deceiver (7:12). As C. S. Lewis famously said,

> There is no halfway house and there is no parallel in other religions. If you had gone to Buddha and asked him: "Are you the Son of Bramah?" He would have said, "My son you are still in

the vale of illusion!" If you had gone to Socrates and asked "are you Zeus?", he would have laughed at you. If you had gone to Mohammad and asked, "Are you Allah?" He would have first rent his clothes and cut off your head. If you had asked Confucius, "Are you heaven?" I think he would probably have said "Remarks which are not in accordance with nature are in bad taste."[50]

Yet at the end of the Gospel, Jesus accepts the worship of Thomas, who says, "My Lord and my God!" (20:28), gently rebuking him for being slow to believe. Indeed, Lewis tells us the one thing we cannot say about Jesus is that he was simply a great moral teacher:

> A man who was merely a man and said the sort of things Jesus said would not be a great moral teacher. He would either be a lunatic—on a level with the man who says he is a poached egg— or else he would be the Devil of Hell. You must make your choice. Either this man was, and is, the Son of God: or else a madman or something worse. You can shut him up for a fool, you can spit at him and kill him as a demon; or you can fall at his feet and call him Lord and God. But let us not come with any patronising nonsense about his being a great human teacher. He has not left that open to us. He did not intend to.[51]

It was precisely these issues, and their life consequences, that the crowds and the authorities were wrestling with on the occasion of Jesus's appearance at this Feast of Tabernacles.

---

50   C. S. Lewis, *Mere Christianity* (London: Fount Collins, 1981), p. 52.
51   Lewis, *Mere Christianity*, p. 52.

Division and dissension (7:14-36)

The focus in these verses is the authenticity of the teaching of Jesus. The dilemma that the crowd faces in assessing Jesus is that, on the one hand, the authority, wisdom and compelling nature of his teaching is self-evident, but on the other, they wonder where it came from, because they know that he has no formal rabbinic education. The question therefore arises: "How did this man get such learning (literally scriptural understanding—"sacred letters"—Greek *grámmata*) without having studied?" (7:15). The answer of course, as Jesus explains, is a hidden but very real source for his teaching. Often Jesus will say that both the words he utters and the works that he performs come from the Father. Thus, Jesus plainly says, "My teaching is not my own, it comes from him who sent me" (7:16). Furthermore, the teaching is self-authenticating, so that by following it, you find out if it is true. In other words, it will prove true when kept. The secret of this self-authenticating truth is that if it is taught not for the aggrandisement of the speaker (in this case Jesus), but for the honour of the one who sent him, then the truth of the teaching will be plain. In other words, the motive for teaching is important, and this is especially true today among contemporary teachers in the Church. If teaching is seen as a way of "gaining a following" or "boosting my self-image" or "raising my profile", although it still might benefit others it will be tarnished, and in time this self-interest will show through. Jesus goes on to say that it is not enough to possess the Law or the Teaching of Moses, or, by implication, his own, unless you keep it. In a moment, Jesus will give a concrete example of a way his hearers fail to keep the Law of Moses. But now he goes one step further and says, "Why are you trying to kill me?" (7:19).

When Jesus lobs this accusation into the midst of the crowd in Jerusalem, quite possibly in the Temple Courts, the temperature rises yet further. Some say, "you are demon-possessed", and others, "who is trying to kill you?" (7:20). Brushing their question aside, Jesus points out the double standards of the Jewish leaders: they are prepared to circumcise on the Sabbath, but they are not prepared to see Jesus make a sick person whole on the same Sabbath (7:23). This leads Jesus to say, "stop judging by mere appearances, and make a right judgement"

(7:24). Such a judgement will be informed by the weightier matters of the Law: compassion, mercy, justice and faithfulness (Matthew 23:23,24). Following this reply, the temperature rises even further, so much so that the authorities begin to seek Jesus's arrest.

Jesus would find it difficult to fill in a modern identity form with its questions about his occupation, place of birth, father's name, etc., as he did not fit normal human categories. And seemingly the groups in Jerusalem during the festival find it similarly difficult to place him. It appears from the next verses (7:25–36) that there is considerable confusion about his identity, something not helped by the teasing and mysterious language he uses. The main groups in this passage appear to be the permanent residents of Jerusalem (see 7:25), the crowds (7:31)— quite probably the pilgrims who swelled the population at festivals like the Feast of Tabernacles—and the Jews, meaning the Jewish leaders (7:35), among whom are the Pharisees. These three distinct groups have their own responses to Jesus.

The Jerusalemites' reasons for questioning Jesus come from the rumours they have heard about him, and their attempts to align him with what they think they know about the Messiah and his origins. They have heard that the authorities want to kill him (7:25), but since they know where Jesus of Nazareth came from, they conclude that he cannot be the Messiah, since they wrongly suppose that the Messiah's origins will be unknown. (See Matthew 2:4–5, where it is reported that the Messiah will come from Bethlehem.) Jesus responds to this in a loud voice while teaching in the Temple. He says he knows his origin is from "him who sent me" (7:29), which is surely a reference to his eternal origin in the Godhead. Provoked, the authorities try to arrest Jesus, but cannot do so because his hour has not yet come. Others, presumably from among the pilgrim crowds, believe in him, recognizing the evidence of his many miracles (7:31).

If some are now believing in him, those who are jealous of him and threatened by his teaching and popularity among the people seek all the more to arrest him. The Pharisees actually send the temple guards to arrest him (7:32), but it is an abortive attempt, because they too are transfixed by his teaching and unable to arrest him (7:45,46). Instead, they find themselves listening to the mysterious teaching that he will only be with them for a short time (more) and that then they will not find him, "for where I am you cannot come" (7:34). Unable to make sense of this statement, the Jews think that Jesus is going to leave Judea and teach the Jewish communities among the Greek Diaspora (7:35). With all this going on, and in the midst of the division among the Jews, Jesus extends one of his great invitations to all people.

The invitation to drink of the Spirit (7:37–52)

On the last and greatest day of this eight-day festival (see Leviticus 23:36), Jesus makes his considered declaration, which deliberately follows a ceremony in which a procession comes from the Pool of Siloam. Water is carried in a golden flagon by the High Priest, accompanied by trumpets, something which has occurred on every previous day. This seven-day ritual of bringing water from Siloam ceases on the eighth day, when there is a solemn culminating sacrifice (see Leviticus 23:36b and Deuteronomy 16:13–17). The feast is a joyous occasion, recalling as it does the water that came from the rock struck by Moses in the wilderness (Exodus 17:6,7); the prophecy of Ezekiel that water would flow in an ever-deeper stream from the Temple (Ezekiel 47); and also the prophecy of Isaiah to draw water from the wells of salvation (Isaiah 12:3). It is on this eighth day, when the water ceremony has ceased, that Jesus stands up, and in a loud voice proclaims that there is another type of water to drink.[52] He cries out, "If anyone is thirsty [spiritually], let him or her come to me and drink. Whoever believes in me, as the Scripture has said, streams of living water will flow from within them" (7:37–38). In one of his editorial asides, John helpfully adds, "By this he meant the Spirit, whom those who believed in him were later to receive" (7:39).

Jesus here is anticipating the gift of the Spirit still to be given, following his passion, as John says (7:39b), and about whom Jesus will teach extensively in the Upper Room Discourse (especially Chapters 14–16). This teaching in the Upper Room is unique to John and once again underlines the Trinitarian nature of his Gospel, as well as the initial

---

52   Morris, *Gospel According to St John*, pp. 419–21.

promise made by the Baptist that Jesus will baptize or immerse people in the Holy Spirit (1:33). The effect of this Spirit-baptism will be that personal spiritual power will open up within them, just as Jesus promises the woman at the well when he says to her, "Everyone who drinks this water will be thirsty again, but whoever drinks the water I give them will never thirst. Indeed, the water I give them will become in them a spring of water welling up to eternal life" (4:13,14). Here in John 7, the Spirit is not so much a gift of personal salvation, but a stream of life-giving, healing power flowing from one person to others, and to the world.

Throughout Christian history people have experienced this blessing and empowering of the Spirit in the way described by Jesus. Basil of Caesarea, who wrote the first book on the Spirit in c.AD 380, said of the Spirit's effect:

> The Spirit illuminates those who have been cleansed from every stain and makes them spiritual by means of communion with himself. When a ray of light falls upon clear and translucent bodies, they are themselves filled with light and gleam with a light from themselves. Just so are the Spirit-bearing souls that are illuminated by the Holy Spirit: they are themselves made spiritual, and they send forth grace to others. Thence comes foreknowledge of the future, understanding of mysteries, apprehension of secrets, distributions of graces, heavenly citizenship, the choirs with angels, unending joy, remaining with God, and the highest object of desire, becoming God.[53]

Likewise, the polymath, inventor and philosopher Blaise Pascal wrote as follows of the night of 23 November 1654, when he had a life-changing experience of God, surely revealed to him by the Spirit, between the hours of 10.30 p.m. and 12.30 a.m.:

---

[53] Basil of Caesarea, *On the Holy Spirit* (Crestwood, NY: SVS Press, 2011), p. 54.

FIRE

GOD of Abraham, GOD of Isaac, GOD of Jacob

Not the God of philosophers and of the learned.

Certitude. Certitude. Feeling. Joy. Peace

God of Jesus Christ.

Your God will be my God (Ruth 1:16)

Forgetfulness of the world and of everything, except GOD.

He can only be found by the ways taught in the Gospel.

Grandeur to the human soul.

Righteous Father, the world has not known you,

    but I have known you (John 17:25)

Joy, Joy, Joy, tears of joy.

We know of this because Pascal wrote it out and sewed the note into the lining of his cloak, where it was later discovered.[54]

Much later, in the nineteenth century, the evangelist D. L. Moody wrote of a revelation he had in New York City: "Oh what a day I cannot describe it, it is almost too sacred an experience to name. I can only say that God revealed himself to me and I had such an experience of his love that I had to ask him to stay his hand."[55]

Such was the authority of Jesus's teaching in the Temple area that the guards sent by the Chief Priests cannot arrest him. Their reason is that, "No one ever spoke the way this man does" (7:46). The attempted arrest is not unlike the later incident in Gethsemane when once again the authority of Jesus prevents the guards from arresting him, and where they even fall to the ground (18:6)! But for now, the temple guards return to the Jewish authorities with their explanation, to receive the harsh condemnation that they too have been "deceived" (7:47). Nicodemus bravely steps forward to object to his compatriots' methods and request a fair hearing for Jesus (7:50,51), but such is the tension among the Jewish

---

[54]   James Connor, *Pascal's Wager: The Man who Played Dice with God* (San Francisco: Harper, 2006), p. 148.

[55]   D. C. K. Watson, *I Believe in Evangelism* (London: Hodder & Stoughton, 1976), p. 182.

leaders that they even berate their fellow leader with heavy sarcasm (7:52).

If the hostility between the Jews (which in John's Gospel means the Jewish authorities) and Jesus is already great, in the next two chapters it will only increase further, until Jesus is forced to leave Jerusalem and his hour has fully come.

CHAPTER 9

Traps, Testimony and True Freedom

John 8:1–59

The conflict between the Jewish leaders and Jesus continues right through this chapter and into the next, and indeed only becomes deeper and more hostile. The initial attempt at an arrest spoken of in Chapter 7 has failed and so now different tactics are employed. Often it appears that the tactics of the Jewish leaders are to discredit Jesus publicly and hence engineer a fall-off in his authority and popularity. Of course, he is more than able to both see through their wiles and see off any such attempts. Furthermore, in this chapter Jesus gives his sixth teaching discourse, concentrating on his precedence over Abraham as the Light of the World.

John 8 begins with an attempt to trap Jesus and involves a live exhibit. (The story is not in all the manuscripts or codices of John's Gospel, however, but since the account is so in keeping with the ministry of Jesus it has been judged authentic.) Presumably this rather sordid and one-sided attempt to catch a woman in an act of adultery has been some time in the making. The woman, quite possibly a prostitute, is seeing a man regularly, and the Jewish leaders hatch a plot to kidnap her *in flagrante* and present her to Jesus in the hope that he would not call for her stoning (an assumption made on the basis of his previous actions). They would then present Jesus to the population as being in breach of the Mosaic Law, which called for punishment of such promiscuity. They pointedly leave the man behind, not bringing him out with the woman, thus showing their insincerity, since he too would have been in breach of the Law. Nevertheless, Jesus, once again teaching in the Temple Courts at some point after the Feast of Tabernacles, is brazenly interrupted by a posse of leaders dragging and humiliating this unfortunate woman as an exhibit in their tawdry attempt at denigrating Jesus.

Jesus is not impressed. From the very start of this incident, he knows what they are doing. They have thrown down their theological gauntlet: "In the Law, Moses commanded us to stone such a woman, now what do you say?" (8:5). Jesus's body language is fascinating throughout this encounter. At first, he does not even look at the Jews, or the woman, but simply draws with his finger in the dirt on the ground. This suggests his anger and contempt at their tactics, and also a profound understanding of their not-so-hidden agenda to malign his reputation and standing. Only as they keep on questioning does Jesus "straighten up" and respond with a one-liner, which, in its own way, is utterly devastating of their cheap ruse: "If any one of you is without sin, let him be the first to throw a stone at her" (8:7). At least they are honest and, beginning with the oldest, they all slink away, leaving the woman alone in front of Jesus. Jesus looks up again, and seeing that the Jews have left, asks her, "Woman, where are they? Has no one condemned you?" When she replies, "no one", Jesus concludes, "Neither do I condemn you. Go now and leave your life of sin" (8:11).

The Jewish leaders' trap has unravelled. An important new principle with regard to Mosaic punishment has been established: only complete innocence qualifies anyone to take part in a stoning, in effect abolishing the practice, for no one is without sin. Furthermore, as John writes earlier, Christ has come not to condemn the world but save it (3:17; 8:11), to liberate people, free them and allow them to fulfil their true humanity. And it is to this notion that we now turn.

Testimony about the Light of the World (8:12–30)

When Jesus resumes his teaching in the Temple area near the Treasury (8:20), after this incident with the woman caught in adultery (8:12), he makes the extraordinary claim that he is the "Light of the World", which is one of the great "I am" sayings of the Gospel. He adds that anyone who follows him, "will never walk in darkness, but will have the light of life" (8:12). This claim is also a continuation of the theme begun in the Prologue that, "In him was life, and that life was the light of all people" (1:4). The claim also resonates with the ceremonies with lights and candelabra that take place in the Feast of Tabernacles, and which commemorate the pillar of fire from Israel's wilderness years (see Exodus 13:21).[56] Indeed, at the end of the feast, the lights of the Temple are extinguished, and it is at this point that Jesus proclaims *himself* the Light of the World. Not surprisingly, the claim to be the Light of the World is like throwing petrol on the fire of the Pharisees' hostility. Immediately, and according to Jewish tradition or custom, they demand that he must have accredited testimony or witnesses to the truth of such a statement. Once again, we are in the particularly Jewish outlook of requiring witnesses to establish theological truths. Yet Jesus responds to the Pharisees by saying that his claim is not unsupported. Firstly, he remarks that his own witness is valid since, unlike the Pharisees (8:14–15), he knows both his origin and destination, but secondly, that his Father also bears witness to him.

As soon as Jesus mentions his Father bearing witness and so corroborating his claim to be the Light of the World, a new line of dispute opens up. A fundamental claim by Jesus, one concerning the very essence of his being, is that he is one with the Father (see especially 14:9–13). Indeed, the identity of Jesus cannot be grasped without reference to the Father who sends him, guides him, and who Jesus seeks to please in all that he says and does (8:29). This remains a mystery to the Jewish leaders, who cannot understand this relationship with the Father of which Jesus has been speaking from the beginning. However, a point of revelation will occur when Jesus says, "when you have lifted up the Son of Man", i.e., when he has been crucified. At that point, Jesus says, "You will know that I am the one I claim to be and that I do nothing on my own but speak just what the Father has taught me" (8:28). Once again Jesus makes it plain that in order to understand who he is, the Jews must understand his relationship with the Father.

A further element of Jesus's teaching here (8:21–24), equally mysterious to the Jews, is that his time with them and the people will be brief, and that following him into the future will require leaving sin and its consequences behind (8:24). In fact, the time that Jesus has left in his

---

56   Morris, *Gospel According to St John*, p. 436.

earthly ministry, or until his crucifixion and resurrection, is probably
only six months. If two Passovers have already gone and this teaching
follows the Feast of Tabernacles in October, it is barely six months until
the next Passover when Jesus will be killed. No wonder, then, that Jesus is
conscious, given this knowledge, that he is "going away, and you will look
for me", and that where he goes, "you cannot come" (8:21). Like John,
Jesus is conscious of the approaching hour when he will be arrested, only
it is not upon him yet (8:20b).

Whose children are you anyhow? (8:31–59)

In many ways, the verses towards the end of John 8 form the centre and
fulcrum of Jesus's conflict with the Jews (again referring to the Jewish
authorities, not the nation). As so often in human affairs, this conflict is
about proper understanding and interpretation of the past. In this case,
the past is defined and characterized by Abraham (in other nations and
systems it might be relationship to Marx, Lenin or Stalin, or in China to
Mao Tse Tung). In the Jewish narrative everything is related to Abraham
and Moses. The question the authorities frequently ask is whether
something conforms to the teaching of these great national leaders. The
question Jesus in effect asks is, "Do the Jews properly understand the
teaching and life of Abraham and Moses, or are they using these two
leaders to repress the people and keep themselves in power?"

The conversation seems to get off to an encouraging start, with Jesus
saying to the Jews who believe in him that freedom comes from truly
being his disciples, and from following the truth of his teaching. Yet this
"believing" does not appear to last long: perhaps it is initial enthusiasm
that quickly fades, like the seed that falls on the path (see Mark 4:4,15).
Nevertheless, Jesus has introduced an enormously important theme to
do with freedom. There are many forms of freedom: political freedom as
in a democracy and the right to choose who governs; freedom of speech;
or freedom to worship how you wish. These are hard-fought freedoms
that do not exist across the globe and are often in danger of being snuffed
out. Jesus is here talking about the most profound of freedoms, the
freedom to become who we are intended to be. He teaches that this is not

possible except in following his commandments: for his service is perfect freedom, his yoke is easy (well-fitting, rather than without cost), and his burden is light (see Matthew 11:30). The truth, and it is a paradox, is that service of Christ is freedom, while serving ourselves is a form of slavery. Or to put it another way, to be a slave or servant is to become free, but to become a slave to our selfish desires or mere human systems is to revert to a form of spiritual slavery. The Jews do not understand this, for they believe that regardless of anything else, as Abraham's descendants, *ipso facto* they are free. It is true that they have left behind slavery of a kind in Egypt (see Exodus 12:31ff.), but serving their own interests puts them back into a form of slavery. They are thus offended by the notion that they can be children of Abraham but in some sense slaves. Furthermore, Jesus's teaching that "everyone who sins is a slave to sin" (8:34), and that no slave has a permanent place in a family household, begs the question, "how then does a person become free?" The answer given by Jesus is that "if the Son sets you free, you will be free indeed" (8:36). This is a freedom that lineal descent from Abraham does not automatically bestow. An act of liberation by the Son is required.

Some years ago, I heard the well-known missionary to Hong Kong Jackie Pullinger talking about a visit to a top-security gaol in Britain. Following her visit, she received the following letter from a high-security prisoner, "I love the Jesus who you helped me to find: the Jesus who is not too big to get his hands dirty and wash the disciples' feet; the Jesus who rolls up his sleeves to help the downcast and poor; the Jesus who stretched out his arms on the cross. Once you have met this Jesus you cannot settle for anyone less." The paradox was that this man would remain in prison for some years, yet inside he had found freedom from the guilt and humiliation of the past.

Jesus goes on to say that although the Jews claim genetic descent from Abraham, they do not resemble him in behaviour or in family likeness. Calling on genetic descent without manifesting the true characteristics of the family is insincere and lacks value. Evidence of this lack of family likeness is shown by the Jews' desire to kill Jesus, who has brought them teaching formed in the Father's presence (8:38). Provokingly, Jesus then says, "you do [rather] what you have heard from your Father" (8:38). But who is their Father if not Abraham? The Jews protest that they are not illegitimate children, but are in direct succession from Abraham, which makes God their Father (8:41).

Jesus contests this claim, making the case that if God were their Father through the lineage of Abraham, they would love him, as the Father has sent him (and of course we know that the Father and Jesus are one; see John 14:9). But since they hate him, the conclusion is that these Jewish leaders "belong to [their] father the devil, and want to carry out [their] father's desires" (8:44). Of the devil Jesus now says, "He was a murderer from the beginning, not holding to the truth, for there is no truth in him. When he lies, he speaks his native language, for he is a liar and the father of lies" (8:44). Furthermore, since Jesus has not lied, but has told the truth, and since they can produce no evidence to the contrary, why don't the Jews believe him?

It is a truism that when people lose an argument or cannot gainsay others, they often resort to abuse. This is what happens now. The Jews call Jesus either a Samaritan (i.e., not a proper Jew, but a hybrid) or demon-possessed. Jesus's reply is to raise the stakes still further. He claims that his Father seeks his glory (8:50), and what is more, "anyone who keeps my word, will never see [taste] death" (8:51). The Jews take even greater exception to this last claim, as it suggests Jesus is greater than Abraham, who did taste death and die. "Are you greater than our father Abraham?" they counter. "He died and so did the prophets. Who do you think you are?" (8:53).

This final question, "Who do you think you are?", is the central one. The Jews have decided Jesus is at most a renegade teacher obsessed with his own importance. Only Jesus now maintains that the Father will glorify him (8:54) and that he knows the Father ("I know him", 8:55). What is more, Abraham rejoiced at the thought of seeing his day. To the objection that no one so young can have seen Abraham, Jesus makes a final claim which enrages them: "I tell you the truth, before Abraham was born, I am!" (8:58). (Here he is taking the divine name of "I am", see Exodus 3:14.)

The claim to be eternally self-existent and present lies at the heart of the claim to divinity. In the context of the Gospel of John, this assertion underscores the claim in the Prologue that Jesus is the eternal Word, with no beginning or end, begotten of the Father. And in the language of the Nicene Creed, Jesus is "one in substance" (*homoousios*) with the Father. He is the Word who pre-existed Abraham, as indeed all created beings, and who takes on flesh in Jesus, born of Mary. He now addresses the Jews who refuse to believe in him, saying that despite their searching of the Scriptures, and the fact that they say they follow Moses and are descended from Abraham, they have been blinded by the devil, whose ways they now follow.

For the Jews, Jesus's claim to be "I am" and to be "before Abraham", not only temporally, but also in status, is blasphemy worthy of stoning. The issue throughout John's Gospel is that Jesus's claims and teaching are either blasphemous or true. This is the hinge of the Gospel, and to believe is to pass from death to life, from darkness to light. We are now about to hear about one who made that transition, literally and spiritually, and who came out of darkness into light, before hearing of another who literally and spiritually passed from death to life. The next three chapters tell of the remaining and culminating signs of the Gospel.

CHAPTER 10

The Man Born Blind

John 9:1–41

The healing of the man born blind appears in the same sequence of events and controversies between Jesus and the Jews that follow the Feast of Tabernacles in John 7. John simply introduces this, the sixth sign of the Gospel, with the phrase, "As he went along . . . " (9:1). But this sign is also connected with Jesus calling himself "the Light of the World" (see 9:5), which in turn is a repetition of his earlier claim in John 8 that he is the Light of the World (8:12). Indeed, the healing of the man born blind is seemingly a sign demonstrating physically that Jesus is the Light of the World, bringing light into the darkness the man has experienced quite literally since birth.

Initially, the appearance of the blind man in their path provokes a brief theological conversation between Jesus and the disciples. The disciples ask, "Rabbi, who sinned, this man or his parents, that he was born blind?" (9:2). The disciples are here giving voice to a common assumption of the time that disability or suffering is the product of sin in the family or individual, either themselves or their ancestors. We see this assumption expressed by Job's Comforters in repeatedly maintaining Job's suffering is the result of his sin (see Job 22:1–11 and 34:1–20), although at the outset of the book of Job, God says to Satan, "Have you considered my servant Job? There is no one on earth like him: he is *blameless and upright, a man who fears God and shuns evil*" (Job 1:8). Nevertheless, the Comforters continue to insist that Job's suffering is the result of his own sin. But here, in reply to the disciples' question about whether this man or his parents sinned, Jesus denies that sin is the cause of the blindness. He is blind so that the work of God might be displayed in his life, Jesus says.

Once again Jesus reiterates that he is the Light of the World and therefore the one to bring light into this man's life, and he and the disciples must now do the Father's work while they have the opportunity. Having acknowledged this broad mandate, Jesus chooses to heal this man through a particular cure, and, it appears, he does so on the Sabbath.

Jesus chooses to heal in a variety of ways in the Gospels. Sometimes he heals with a word, sometimes at a distance, and sometimes through a particular action. In this case, Jesus mixes saliva with clay or earth and creates a paste which he puts on the man's eyes (see also Mark 8:22–26). Some of the Church Fathers read into this a symbol of the divine mixed with the earthly to form human life (Genesis 2:7). By this symbolic method of placing paste on the man's eyes, Jesus restores the power of sight.[57] Having placed the paste on the man's eyes, Jesus commands him to go and wash in the Pool of Siloam on the west side of the Temple Mount above the Kidron Valley. Jesus thus gives the man something to do which involves both obedience and faith. He goes, does as he is told, and goes home "seeing" (9:7).

There now begins the first steps of an enquiry into the identity of the man who has been healed and the identity of the person who has healed him. So laborious and convoluted does this enquiry become that it provokes the feistiness of the man born blind, who emerges as one of the more plain-speaking characters of the Gospels, on a par with the Syro-Phoenician woman (see Mark 7:24–30). At first the man's neighbours get talking and ask, "Isn't this the same man who used to sit and beg?" Some think it is, but some don't. The man then acknowledges that he is the self-same beggar and has been cured after washing mud from his eyes in the Pool of Siloam on the instruction of a man known as Jesus (9:11). Seeking further proof, they ask where Jesus is now, but the healed man does not know. At this point, the investigation starts to take the form of a religious enquiry, along with the charge or suspicion of Sabbath-breaking.

---

57   Morris, *Gospel According to St John*, p. 481.

A full-scale investigation

Given the existing tension between the Jewish authorities and Jesus, this healing of the man born blind further fuels the fire of their antipathy. It seems that the neighbours, sensing the making of a controversy, bring the now-healed man to the Pharisees (9:13). The scope of the furore is extended when the Pharisees learn that Jesus healed the man on the Sabbath, which they consider work, and hence banned by the Law (see Matthew 23:23,24). After all, Jesus has made mud with clay and spittle, and has applied this mixture to the man's eyes. Furthermore, the man has then gone and washed, and has received his sight. The Pharisees view this as a clear contravention of the Sabbath laws, which means Jesus cannot have been sent by God (9:16). Nor can he be a prophet, which the man born blind claims (9:17b), nor is he the Messiah. Not content to believe that the man was ever really blind, the Pharisees send for his parents to identify him. The parents, who may well have been ordinary Jerusalemites, are somewhat cowed by the inquisition of the Pharisees. Although they are prepared to say the blind man is their son, they are not prepared to speculate about how or by whom he was healed, because they fear being put out of the synagogue for supporting Jesus as the Messiah. "How he can see now or who opened his eyes, we don't know," they reply. "Ask him. He is of age; he will speak for himself" (9:21). At this point the Pharisees summon the man for a second cross-examination.

This second interview (9:24) begins with the pious injunction, "Give glory to God", which is a euphemism for "You had better watch out as God himself is watching." The man is unimpressed by this bit of sham piety. The Pharisees then give their verdict, one he is supposed to concur with, saying, "We know this man is a sinner." The Jewish leaders thus reach their conclusion before hearing the evidence! In response, the man born blind gives a feisty, down-to-earth and famous reply, "Whether he is a sinner or not, I don't know. One thing I do know. I was blind but now I see!" (9:25). Pressed to go over the details of his healing again and explain how it was done, the man goads the Pharisees, saying, "I have told you already and you did not listen. Why do you want to hear it again? Do you want to become his disciples too?" (9:27). At this they are riled, protesting that they are the true disciples of Moses; they are not the disciples of this man of uncertain origin (9:29). With vaulting irony and invective, the man born blind castigates them: "You don't know where he comes from, yet he opened my eyes" (9:30). Indeed, only those blessed by God can open the eyes of the blind, so the conclusion must be that Jesus, far from being a sinner, is sent by God (9:31–33). At this, the Pharisees and the leaders of the Jews lose all patience and throw the formerly blind man out of their presence, and most probably from the synagogue community of their district of Jerusalem also.

Jesus hears that the man has been ejected from the synagogue and goes to find him. When he does so, he completes the cure by asking the man if he believes in the Son of Man, a title most frequently used by Jesus of himself, but originating from the divine figure in the book of Daniel (see Daniel 7:13; 10:5,6). As with the woman at the well (4:26), Jesus now discloses himself as the Son of Man and immediately the man gives his worship (Greek: *prosekuneō*) and belief (Greek: *pisteuō*). This combination of *belief* and *worship* lies at the heart of *the right human response to Christ*, the Incarnate Word. And throughout the Gospel different people give it: Nathanael, the woman at the well and Thomas among them.

Jesus now summarizes the whole incident: both the healing of the man and the fierce condemnation of the Jewish leaders. His presence is like judgement: to those who are blind and who now believe, he gives sight as the Light of the World (9:5); but those who claim to see but do not believe remain spiritually blind. Their obtuse reaction only worsens their spiritual blindness. Some Pharisees who are with him object, sensing that Jesus is passing judgement on *their* blindness (9:40). Then Jesus confirms that since they claim to see without truly believing in him, they are in fact blind. Here his words are a warning to the self-assured, and a plea for self-examination and true humility.

This sixth sign of the Gospel now leads into the seventh and last discourse of the Gospel and the statement that Jesus is the Good Shepherd.

CHAPTER 11

The Good Shepherd

John 10:1–42

One of the most common sights in Palestine is still that of a shepherd with
his sheep, and sometimes with goats as well. Since it is such a common
image and because there are many parallels between shepherding and
caring for the flock of God, it is no wonder that it was a popular and
telling spiritual metaphor throughout Israel's history, although at first
the Pharisees do not understand the significance of Jesus's allegory (see
verse 6).

This is the seventh and last discourse of this the first part of the
Gospel, in which Jesus describes himself as the Good Shepherd. The
discourse also contains the fourth and fifth of the "I am" sayings in
John's Gospel. Already in the first part of the Gospel we have had Jesus
describing himself as "the Bread of Life" (6:35,48), as "the Light of the
World" (9:5) and as preceding Abraham ("before Abraham was born,
I am", 8:58). In this section of teaching—his seventh and last public
discourse (after Chapter 11, all Jesus's teaching is private and directed
solely at his disciples)—Jesus takes the image of pastoral leadership from
the metaphor of the shepherd frequently found in the Old Testament. In
fact, in this discourse he calls himself both the door or "gate" of the sheep
(10:7) and "the Good Shepherd" (10:11,14). There are only two more "I
am" sayings to come: in John 11, where Jesus says he is "the resurrection
and the life" (11:25), and in John 14 in the Upper Room discourse, where
he says he is "the way and the truth and the life" (14:6).

The image of the shepherd to describe pastoral leadership is found
frequently in the Old Testament, not least in Psalm 23, where the Lord is
described as the Shepherd. The metaphor is often also used in criticism

of Israel's leaders, who have turned out to be false shepherds. This is particularly true in Ezekiel, where the prophet says, "I am against the shepherds and will hold them accountable for my flock. I will remove them from tending the flock so that the shepherds can no longer feed themselves. I will rescue my flock from their mouths, and it will no longer be food for them" (Ezekiel 34:10; see also Isaiah 56:9–12; Jeremiah 23:1–4; 25:32–38 and Zechariah 11). The Old Testament prophet Micah promised a new leader, however, a Messiah who would come from Bethlehem and who would "stand and shepherd Israel" (see Micah 5:1–4). He would be the perfect shepherd. Now, following on from the healing of the man born blind, Jesus claims the title of the Shepherd of Israel and of those others who will be called into his fold.

The teaching begins with an allegory the disciples do not immediately understand, but which Jesus then further expands. Perhaps it is in view of the tension between the Jews and Jesus—in which they have sought to arrest or, alternatively, stone him (see 7:32b, 8:59)—that Jesus turns his thoughts to the idea of the Good Shepherd, the one who has the best interests of the flock at heart and whose Kingdom is about to be opened to a wider group than the Jews alone. Whatever the exact train of thought bringing him to this point, Jesus contrasts leaders or shepherds who have the true interests of the flock at heart with those who are seeking to jeopardize the flock's wellbeing.

The ministry of the Good Shepherd (10:1–21)

In the first section of this allegory, Jesus is at pains to show that the sheep are vulnerable to various types of leadership and exploitation. The true shepherd cares for the sheep, but there are others who come to damage or destroy the flock. In Palestine at the time, sheep are led by their shepherd to find pasture and are kept in strong pens made of mud walls with an opening for the gate. The shepherd normally enters by the gate (10:2), but an intruder or thief climbs over the wall (10:1b). Furthermore, the shepherd lies down across the entrance to the pen at night, and for this reason can be considered the gate of the sheep (10:7).

Sheep have sensitive voice recognition—a faculty nowadays associated with electronic security devices used for ascertaining identity in banking or other forms of commerce. Jesus says that the true shepherd is readily identified by his voice, and so too is any watchman employed to maintain security at a pen (10:3). Equally, the shepherd has true knowledge of each individual sheep, calling them by an affectionate name (10:3b). The sheep follow the shepherd because they know his voice and are content to be led by him, knowing that he has their best interests at heart (10:4). By contrast, they will not follow a stranger, but will instead run away (10:5).

As Jesus develops this analogy, he brings it to a critical juncture, comparing himself with other religious leaders, either contemporary with him, or who came before him. These individuals are not "interested in the wellbeing of the sheep but in their own advantage" and must refer to the religious establishment called by John "the Jews", individuals who sought to rob people of their dignity and freedom and prevent them from heeding the true shepherd.[58] They are termed "thieves and robbers" (10:8), and behind them is "the thief" whose intent is "to steal, kill and destroy" (10:10). By contrast, Jesus comes that the sheep "might have life, and have it to the full" (10:10b). This abundant life (*zoē*) is the gift of God, and in John's Gospel is consistently the outcome of faith or belief.

Yet for the Good Shepherd there is a great cost, and in the next part of the parable this cost is spelt out. The Good Shepherd must be prepared to lay down his life for the sheep, and one of the chief distinguishing marks between the true shepherd and the hired hand is that when trouble comes and the wolf attacks, the hired hand runs away because he has no real interest in the sheep (10:12,13).

Having drawn this distinction, in the next verses Jesus reiterates his calling and his own role as the Good Shepherd (10:14–18). He reaffirms his close relationship with the sheep: they know him and he knows them. Indeed, that knowledge is potentially as close as that of Father and Son (10:15,17). The sacrifice the Good Shepherd must make will further endear him to his Father (10:17). It will be a free decision made out of love for the sheep and loving obedience to the Father. Jesus will lay down his life, but he has the power to take it up again, such is the authority

---

58 Morris, *Gospel According to St John*, p. 506.

(Greek: *exousia*) that he has (10:18b). No other person but the incarnate Son of God has the authority to lay down his life and take it up again, which is the charge or commission received from his Father (10:18b). The effect of this sacrifice will be that all people may come into this fold, and the flock will be greatly extended to include both Jew and Gentile (see Ephesians 3:6). The Gentiles are referred to as the sheep that are not yet part of the same sheep pen, but which must be brought in so that "there shall be one flock and one shepherd" (10:16). As before, this teaching divides his listeners, with some saying he is raving mad (10:20) and others saying that they aren't the words of a demon or madman, for a madman is not able to open the eyes of the blind (10:21).

A time for decision: The Feast of the Dedication

Once again John's Gospel is built around a Jewish festival. This time it is not one of the three original festivals given by Moses for the people to celebrate annually: i.e., Passover, Pentecost (or the Jewish Feast of Weeks, Shavuot, celebrated 50 days after Passover and for the wheat harvest) or the Feast of Tabernacles. Much later, and following the Maccabean Revolt (167–160 BC) against the Seleucid King Antiochus IV Epiphanes, who had desecrated the Temple, the Temple was rededicated and the Feast of Hanukkah or Dedication was thereafter kept in December, or on the 25th of the Jewish month of Kislev. It is during this feast, which lasted eight days, and was being held some 200 years after its inception, that Jesus is found walking in Solomon's colonnades around the Temple and is once more asked by the Jews who "surround" him (10:24), but now in a more threatening manner, to fully reveal his identity: "If you are the Christ, tell us plainly" (10:24) they say.

Jesus's reply is, in effect, that they have already been told. They have been told through the miracles granted by the Father and which are signs of Jesus's Messiahship (10:25). Furthermore, there is a sense in which those who are already part of his flock, by virtue of believing, have an insider's knowledge that he is truly the Messiah. This of course will become even clearer once the Holy Spirit has been given and received (14:20). "Those who are already in the flock, my sheep, are known by the Son, they follow him and are assured of eternal life that cannot be taken away from them" (10:27–28). There is also an indication here that this flock, which has been given by the Father to the Son, is the most significant community in the world. That is, if we understand verse 29 as saying, "What my Father has given me is greater than all", rather than the variant reading that runs, "the Father is greater than all". The first and probably the original reading is more likely to be the one meant, as a point about the Father being greater than all would not have been news. Whereas the reality of this new community of Jew and Gentile being created by the Father as the most significant community on earth was startling and radical. This reality accords, however, with the Apostle Paul's teaching in Ephesians where he says: "His intent was that now, through the church [the flock of God] the manifest wisdom of God should be made known to the rulers and authorities in the heavenly realms, according to his eternal purpose which he accomplished in Christ Jesus our Lord" (Ephesians 3:10,11). If it is offensive to the Jews that this new community comprising Jew and Gentile, granted to the Son by the Father, is now the future, Jesus's final saying is blasphemy to them. He claims, "I and the Father are one." There are few clearer statements of the co-divinity of Father and Son, or to put it in the terms of the Nicene Creed, that the Son is of the same substance as the Father (10:30). The Jews at once pick up stones to throw at him. Jesus responds ironically with the question, "I have shown you many great miracles (Greek: *erga*) from the Father. For which of these do you stone me?" (10:32). They reply that they are stoning him not for the miracles but for blasphemy, for claiming to be God himself!

Jesus now embarks on an interesting line of argument. Referring to the Hebrew Scriptures, and in particular a Psalm which he calls the Torah, or "your Law", he points his listeners to the phrase "sons of the Highest" used by the Psalmist (here Asaph) of the judges who failed to rule against the unjust and the wicked, and who in this failure were unlike their Heavenly Father, the one who "defends the cause of the weak and fatherless and maintains the rights of the poor and oppressed". If Scripture, perhaps ironically, calls these unjust judges, "Sons of the Most High" (Psalm 82:6), what is so wrong with Jesus calling himself the Son of God, sent into the world by the Father himself? (John 10:36b). Jesus then expresses the hope that as they consider his works or miracles, they too will receive an epiphany and come to believe that "the Father is in me and I in the Father" (10:38). This complete mutuality between Father and Son is only expressed in St John's Gospel, making it unique in this respect, and strengthening the argument that this really is the Gospel of the Trinity.

Although the shepherd image used by Jesus is one of the most loved and enduring, originally it was set in the context of ongoing and increasing hostility between the Jewish leadership and Jesus. In this analogy, Jesus describes false leaders as those who do not come in by the gate but climb over the wall (10:1), and who are like hirelings that run away when there is trouble (10:12). On the other hand, he says that he has come to bring life in all its fullness, and that his sheep recognize his voice and follow him. He in turn leads them out to pasture, and, supremely, will lay down his life for them, as commissioned by the Father (10:17,18), only to pick it up again in his resurrection. Through this shepherding he will bring in sheep from another fold (the Gentiles). In this discourse, Jesus also repeatedly claims to be one with the Father (10:30,38b) who has given him the flock (10:29). In all, the image of a shepherd is a remarkable and enduring model of pastoral leadership which is life-giving and life-preserving. Yet despite all this, Jesus is forced to leave Jerusalem, as hostility has increased to such a pitch that his life is constantly in danger, and to await the right time, indeed "the hour" of his arrest, passion and crucifixion.

The final verses of this chapter find Jesus once again outside Jerusalem and waiting for the right time to be delivered into the hands of the Jewish and Roman authorities. He strategically retreats to the Jordan, and to the place where the Baptist had baptized early on. Many people come to him and believe (10:42). Jesus waits there for the right time to re-enter Jerusalem, but one final sign unfolds very near the city, at Bethany, and this is the raising of Lazarus.

CHAPTER 12

The Raising of Lazarus

John 11:1–57

We come in this chapter to the climax of Jesus's public ministry as recorded by John, and also to the end of the first part of the Gospel, before moving into the chapters leading up to the Passion. It really is a climactic chapter: it has the most dramatic of all the seven signs—the raising of Lazarus from the dead; one of the greatest of the "I am" sayings of Jesus—"I am the resurrection and the life" (11:25); and the clearest evidence of the humanity and divinity of Jesus. As well as this, it has the most touching conversation between Jesus, Martha and Mary: each responding to the untimely death of Lazarus in their own very personal way.

The prelude to a final act of power (11:1–16)

In these verses, John sets the scene for the forthcoming sign. Lazarus, who is clearly loved by Jesus, is reported sick in Bethany (11:1,3). Lazarus is the brother of Martha and Mary, the latter identified as the sister who pours precious perfume on Jesus and wipes his feet with her hair (11:2; 12:2,3). The family is well known to Jesus, and it seems that he has often stayed with them (see Luke 10:38–42). The sisters seek to inform Jesus that Lazarus has become ill, and know how to get a message through to him. It is clear that Lazarus is gravely ill, but it appears also that Jesus knows the eventual outcome of this sickness from the start; that it will not (finally) end in death, although Lazarus will die, and, as we shall see, this illness will glorify Jesus and reveal his inner character.

If Jesus's foreknowledge of events is a preliminary sign of his divine power, it is more than matched by his feelings of human love towards Lazarus, Martha and Mary. Twice we are told in the opening verses that Jesus loves this family (11:3,5). Written into both that knowledge and love there is a paradox, however, suggested by the words, "Yet when he heard that Lazarus was sick, he stayed where he was two more days" (11:6). In that little word "yet" there is the consciousness that Jesus does not act as a mere mortal. He loves the family deeply, but he also knows the eventual outcome and the Father's will for Lazarus, and the glory that this will bring to the Son (11:4). The outcome is that Jesus stays where he is for *two more days* and does not hasten to Bethany as might have been expected (see 11:21).

Then, without explanation, Jesus tells the disciples that they must return to Judea, where both Jerusalem and Bethany are found. Not knowing then of the death of Lazarus, the disciples wonder if returning to Judea, where recently Jesus has been so fiercely opposed, is wise. They say, "But Rabbi, a short while ago the Jews tried to stone you" (11:8). Jesus gives an enigmatic reply that while there is still light, or a window of opportunity for good work, then it should be taken, for when darkness comes there will be no further opportunity to work. It is at this point that Jesus reveals his true motive for returning to Judea: "Our friend Lazarus has fallen asleep; but I am going there to wake him up" (11:11). Once more Jesus is speaking enigmatically, at the same time underlining the fact that, for Jesus, death for the believer is like falling asleep and should hold no ultimate fear. Explaining his term for death, Jesus then states clearly that Lazarus is dead (11:14), and that for his disciples' sake he is glad that he is not there so that they might see for themselves the sign which is to come. At that moment, Thomas, in an act of bravado or desperation, says, "let us also go, that we might die with him" (11:16). It seems that by temperament Thomas swings from daring to doubt, but it does appear also that he knows a violent climax is coming.

A conversation with the sisters (11:17–44)

There are few more touching conversations in the Bible than these between Jesus and the sisters, Martha and Mary, so different in many ways but now so united by faith and grief. The context for the opening conversation between Jesus and Martha, the older sister, is well established by John. By the time Jesus arrives at Bethany, just a short distance from Jerusalem, Lazarus has been dead four days (11:17). It seems that Jesus is as much as three days' journey from Bethany when he realizes in his spirit that Lazarus has died (11:11). Because Bethany is close to Jerusalem, and because the family is well known and respected, many Jews have come from Jerusalem to comfort them in their bereavement. At some point, Martha hears that Jesus is near the village. In fact, Jesus has waited outside the village, not wishing to be caught up with the crowds of mourners. He wants to talk to the sisters alone, and then afterwards come to the tomb.

The sisters went to him separately, in keeping with their characters. We know from other passages in Scripture that the sisters have markedly different personalities. Martha is typically an older sister, perhaps the oldest in the family, and she has the demeanour of one: responsible, conscientious to a fault, active and resourceful. When in the past Jesus and his disciples turn up, perhaps unexpectedly, it is she who busies herself in the kitchen to produce a meal while somewhat resenting her younger sister's rapt concentration on Jesus's presence and words (Luke 10:40). Jesus then says to Martha, "Martha, Martha, [using her name twice to break through her anxious self-absorption] you are worried and upset about many things, but only one thing is needed. Mary has chosen what is better, and it will not be taken away from her" (Luke 10:41,42). Now in her grief Martha acts completely in character. She is *actively* going out of the house to meet Jesus. She is *directly* saying, "Lord if you had been here my brother would not have died" (11:21) with the implied criticism that if Jesus had not delayed, he might have healed Lazarus from his sickness. But Jesus has a greater miracle in mind, and indeed Martha declares her trust in him still, saying, "I know that even now God will give you whatever you ask" (11:22). Here is faith which has not been much in evidence in Jerusalem (see 8:19), and which springs from an implicit understanding of the deep relationship between the

Father and the Incarnate Son. Jesus now makes a promise of immense proportions that goes beyond their mutual understanding that Lazarus will rise again on the last day (11:23,24): "I am the resurrection and the life. He who believes in me will live, even though he dies; and whoever lives and believes in me will never die. Do you believe this?" (11:25,26). It is one of the greatest "I am" sayings of the Gospel, in which Jesus reverses the reality and consequences of death, replacing death with resurrection and life. In response, Martha makes an unequivocal statement of faith: "Yes Lord, I believe that you are the Christ, the Son of God, who was to come into the world" (11:27). After this, and quite possibly full of hope, she goes to fetch her sister.

It might be fancy, but there seems to be a particular and special connection between Mary and Jesus. It is she who is content to sit at his feet (Luke 10:39) and is commended for doing so. It is she who anoints him with highly expensive perfume and wipes his feet with her hair (12:3). It is she Jesus asks for, understandably, having spoken with her sister Martha (11:28). And it is Mary's grief that deeply moves him (11:33). They have that almost indefinable human connection which is part of the mystery of being human and reflects a mutual empathy.

When Mary meets Jesus, who is still outside the village, she is followed by anxious mourners who think that she has gone to weep at her brother's tomb. When she finds Jesus at the edge of the village, she typically falls at his feet and repeats the words that her sister has also said, "Lord, if you had been here, my brother would not have died" (11:32). Touched by her distress and that of the Jews accompanying her, we are told by John that Jesus is "deeply moved in spirit" (literally groans, as in Romans 8:22–23), and asks "where have you put him?" Once again in this Gospel the response is "come and see" (cf. 1:39,46; 4:29; 11:34; 20:27). At this Jesus weeps, overcome by the raw emotion of Mary and the others. Moved by their sorrow in the face of death and loss, he expresses his full humanity and deep resentment of the power of death in human life, while at the same time he knows the great sign he is about to deliver.

What we have in this moment is the mystery of Jesus's humanity and divinity. In his mind, he knows that his Father has given him a great work to perform which will display the glory of God and the truth that he is "the resurrection and the life". But in his emotions, equally divine and human, Jesus is moved by the sense of loss in the sisters, and particularly in Mary, and by his friend Lazarus who has become subject to death. All these feelings impinge on his being and we are told quite simply that "Jesus wept" (11:35): the shortest verse in the Bible. And yet this expression of the human Jesus is set against the awesome divine power about to be displayed in calling forth the dead man from the tomb, still wrapped in his grave clothes. The scene remains for artists one of the great subjects of the New Testament, along with the nativity, crucifixion and resurrection. *The Raising of Lazarus* by Sebastiano Piombo, assisted by the mature Michelangelo, painted between 1516 and 1519, was the first picture to be obtained by the National Gallery in London in 1824. However, no one describes the mystery at the heart of Jesus's humanity and divinity with greater perception than one of the Cappadocian Fathers, Gregory Nazianzen, who, in his orations in the Anastasia Chapel in Constantinople in AD 379, said:

> He is stoned, yet not hit; he prays, yet he hears prayer. He weeps, yet he puts an end to weeping. He asks where Lazarus is laid—he was man; yet he raises Lazarus—he was God. He is sold, and cheap was the price—thirty pieces of silver; yet he buys back the world at the mighty cost of his own blood. A sheep, he is led to the slaughter—yet he shepherds Israel and now the whole world as well. A lamb, he is dumb—yet he is "Word", proclaimed by the "voice of one crying in the wilderness". He is weakened, wounded—yet he cures every disease and every weakness. He is brought up to the tree and nailed to it—yet by the tree of life he restores us.[59]

On account of his humanity and his divinity marvellously combined in the mystery of a single person, Jesus both weeps for Lazarus and his family, friends, and indeed humanity, but also prepares for a mighty act of divine power of raising from the dead. With tears literally in his eyes, Jesus asks, "where have you laid him?" (11:34). And the mealy-mouthed

---

59   Gregory of Nazianzus, "Oration 29: On the Son", in *On God and Christ* (Crestwood, NY: SVS Press, 2002), pp. 87–8.

critics, unaware of what he is about to do, complain, "Could not he who opened the eyes of the blind man have kept this man from dying?" (11:37). In fact, by delaying his arrival until after the death of Lazarus, Jesus will do something far more wonderful.

Jesus is brought once again groaning (the Greek *embrimáomai* literally means snorting, as in a horse; or we might say choking back the tears, probably of indignation and anger, at the encroachment of death in human life). Whether Jesus has any premonition of his own death and being laid in a tomb, we do not know, but quite possibly. Lazarus's tomb is similar: cut into rock and with a large stone at the mouth (11:38). Jesus orders the stone removed and Martha, practical as ever, objects that "by this time there is a bad odour for he has been there four days" (11:39). Jesus responds by reiterating what he has said earlier, "If you believed, you would see the glory of God" (11:40). The stone is taken away and then Jesus prays to the Father in a way that shows his unity of will and purpose with the Father and their joyful fellowship, but that also underlines to the bystanders that he has been sent by the Father into the world (11:42) and that he is the eternal Word made flesh. As John puts it in the Prologue, the overture to this Gospel, "No one has ever seen God, but God the One and Only, who is at the Father's side, has made him known." Here Jesus is making known the character and will of the Father and the Godhead. In this sign, the Father and the Son are to be revealed as life-giving (1:4; 11:42).

Having prayed to his Father, Jesus draws close to the rock tomb and, significantly, addresses the dead man, his friend Lazarus, calling him forth from death to life. In an evident parallel to the creation narrative of Genesis 1, in which God says "let there be Light" and "there was light" (Genesis 1:3), Jesus now addresses the lifeless man to restore life. The principle here is that the Word speaks and what is commanded comes forth. The Gospel begins with the statement, which is a parallel to Genesis 1, that the Word, like the Father, is from the beginning; but now the Word chooses to take on flesh to restore the very life which he had created at first: "For without him nothing was made that has been made" (1:3).

Jesus calls out in a loud voice, as on the last day of the feast offering the water of life at the Feast of Tabernacles (7:37): "Lazarus, come out!" This strikes the reader not only as a call to life and a call from death, but also a command *for* death to release him into restored life. The very next verses record eventful facts that can only be found in this Gospel: "The dead man came out, his hands and feet wrapped with strips of linen, and a cloth around his face" (11:44). What will later be left behind by the Risen Christ in the empty tomb (see 20:6,7) must here be taken off by others. Jesus says, "Take off the grave clothes and let him go" (11:44b). Whereas the resurrection of Jesus marks the beginning of a whole new epoch of life, the raising of Lazarus is to a restored life, although not to a whole new way of being, which will be resurrection life. As with the healing of Jairus's daughter, who is also brought back to life (Mark 5:40–43), Jesus does not forget what is practical and needful in the wonder of the miracle. To him they are all of a piece: God's care for his creation.

Response to the raising of Lazarus (11:45–57)

As one might expect from the Gospel narrative so far, the response to the raising of Lazarus, and to Jesus's role in particular, is mixed. Many Jews believe in him (11:45), but others report on what they have witnessed to the Pharisees, who in turn respond to this latest miracle as though it is a crisis. The Chief Priests and the Pharisees call a meeting of the Sanhedrin no less, the highest religious court in the land and responsible for the religious rule of the people, to discuss what to do about Jesus. The gist of their argument is that if they let Jesus go on like this, performing such signs and thereby suggesting that he is the Messiah, it will lead to "everyone believing in him" (11:48) and the effect will be that the Romans, fearing a religious insurrection, will destroy the Temple and attack the nation. In fact, this does happen later, but as a consequence of a Jewish rebellion against Roman rule in AD 66, with the Temple destroyed by Roman legions under Titus in AD 70. With this fear expressed in the Sanhedrin, the Jewish High Priest, Caiaphas, in an almost involuntary way, and guided by the Spirit, says: "You do not realize that it is better for you that one man die for the people than that the whole nation perish" (11:50). Although the High Priest is suggesting that it is more expedient that one man be removed than the whole nation be put in jeopardy, the saying is later understood as a prophecy that it is necessary for one man to die for the people, rather than for the whole nation to perish. In other words, it is an unwitting prophecy that Jesus should die *on behalf of all people*, including the Jewish nation. Indeed, just as the Spirit came upon Saul (1 Samuel 10:6–13) and he prophesied, so likewise the Spirit comes upon the High Priest, Caiaphas, who unwittingly prophesies that Jesus will die in the place of his people (11:51–53). At this moment they finally decide on and plot the death of Jesus (11:53).

From then on, sensing this change of events and the quickening of the High Priests' purpose to kill him, Jesus no longer moves about publicly among the Jews but withdraws to a village called Ephraim, where he quietly waits (11:54). Jerusalem is beginning to fill with people for the Jewish Feast of Passover, a time when the population doubles in size, with Jews coming from all over Palestine and the Diaspora to prepare for the festival. As on other occasions (7:11,12,25ff.), the people keep looking for Jesus, wondering if he will show himself at the feast. They want to see him, and the Chief Priests and Pharisees want to find him so that they might arrest him. There is no doubt that a crisis is fast approaching, and the long-awaited "hour" is almost upon Jesus (11:57). The raising of Lazarus has further raised the temperature of the conflict between Jesus and the authorities; the events leading towards Jesus's passion and death must now take place. The time has come.

CHAPTER 13

The Turning Point

John 12:1–50

The first 11 chapters of John's Gospel present the public ministry of Jesus through the prism of the incarnation: the eternal pre-existent Word taking on flesh through Mary and then displaying to the world the glory of the One and Only who forever dwells with the Father (1:14). These opening 11 chapters are based around seven signs and seven discourses, including several memorable conversations with, among others, Nicodemus and the woman at the well. The great call to all humanity issued by Jesus is to believe in the Son of God and through him in the Father who sent him. In this way, people may come into the light, enjoy life, pass from condemnation to life, and experience God's grace and love. All this is set within increasing conflict with the Jewish authorities, which comes to a head in Chapters seven to 11. And these conflicts with the Jewish leaders generally occur around the great Jewish festivals in Jerusalem.

Chapter 12 begins the transition from the public ministry of Jesus, coming as it does to a crescendo in Chapter 11 with the raising of Lazarus, to the lead-up to his passion and crucifixion. After the raising of Lazarus, it is the settled policy of the High Priest to put Jesus to death so that the Romans will not remove the Jewish authorities' own power because of their failure to check a popular religious movement which Jesus heads (11:48–53). It is in this context that the final week of Jesus's earthly life begins in John 12. It is worth underlining that John uses almost half of his Gospel to describe the events and the teaching surrounding this period leading up to his crucifixion.

The anointing at Bethany

After the raising of Lazarus and the growing hostility from the establishment, Jesus retreats to a more secluded area near the desert, to a village called Ephraim (11:54), but as the time of Passover draws near, he decides to return to Jerusalem. He knows it will be his final week. Six days before the Passover, he returns to Bethany and to the home of Lazarus, newly raised from the dead. Not surprisingly, a dinner is given in his honour by the family and friends. As usual, Martha serves (12:2). Lazarus, with a story to tell, reclines at the table with Jesus, while his sister Mary, in keeping with her exuberant and adoring nature, pours a pint of pure nard (spikenard) on Jesus's feet. (In Mark's Gospel, a similar incident with different details occurs: see Mark 14:1–11. It is hard to say if this is a separate incident in the same village, or the same incident differently reported.) What is true of both accounts is that the perfume is so expensive that it could have been sold for 300 denarii (*triakosiōn dēnaríōn*), and Judas advocates that, rather than being lavished on Jesus, it could be sold and the money given to the poor.

Judas's concern for the poor, however, is not genuine, for he is a thief who keeps the common purse. If the perfume is sold and the money placed in the common purse, Judas would be able to help himself. Jesus makes two points about Mary's action. First, she should be left alone and not harassed, since there is a divine compulsion in her action and it will serve as an example in the future. Secondly, it is preparation for his burial. It is an act of love and worship, but also a prophetic action that, possibly unbeknown to her, prepares Jesus for his burial (12:7). Furthermore, Jesus makes the point that the poor will always be present, but he will be there only for the briefest of time.

At the same time, the crowd, who seem like a milling group of paparazzi, have discovered where Jesus is. Hearing that he is at the home of Lazarus in Bethany, the Chief Priests decide to extend their purge to Lazarus as well, since so many are going over to Jesus because of him (12:9–11). In many ways, these events, recorded early on in this chapter of transition, set the scene for the week and for the passion of Jesus.

The triumphal entry into Jerusalem (12:12-19)

In John's reckoning, Jesus rides triumphantly into Jerusalem five days before his crucifixion on Friday, making this entrance to the city the first day of the Jewish week (see 12:1 and 12:12, "the next day"), or our Sunday. By now the city is full of pilgrims who have come from across the Diaspora. They have, it seems, heard about Jesus and the claim he is the Messiah, and want to see him for themselves; indeed, they are ready to greet him with praise.

Unlike the Synoptic Gospels, where an account is given of the procuring of a donkey and a colt, the foal of a donkey (see Matthew 21:1-3, Mark 11:1-3 and Luke 19:28-31), John proceeds directly to the entry into Jerusalem. He later tells us simply that Jesus has found a donkey to ride (12:14). Taking palm branches (*tà baia tōn phoinikōn*, branches of palm trees), a traditional welcome for a ruler or king, the crowd lay them down in the path of Jesus's procession. They shout repeatedly, at the same time, words of acclamation. *Hosanna* is the transliteration of an Aramaic or Hebrew word meaning "God save him" (not unlike the British national anthem that begins "God save our Gracious King"). Furthermore, they shout words from Psalm 118:25-26: "Blessed is he who comes in the name of the Lord!", and add their own words, "Blessed is the King of Israel" (12:13).

Although there is a sense of coronation about this entry into Jerusalem, there is still something restrained in John's particular telling of it. For John, the coronation or glorification of Jesus is reserved for his being lifted up on the cross, and this entry into Jerusalem is essentially something humble, spontaneous and low-key. Indeed, the nature of the kingship of Jesus is manifest here. He does not arrive on a charger, or a white horse, in a chariot, or with a military escort of helmeted troops. He comes instead on a donkey, with a motley band of supporters, with no outriders and a very uncertain future. John, like the other Gospel writers, understands this entrance to be the fulfilment of Zechariah's prophecy that Israel's king will come seated on a donkey (see 12:15 and Zechariah 9:9). He is the servant, a humble king coming to his own people in their historic and capital city.

John then outlines the response to this event from two directions: the disciples and the Pharisees. The disciples, according to John, do not understand the significance of the occasion. Only after Jesus is "glorified" do they realize that he is fulfilling prophecy in his ride into Jerusalem in humble triumph. What the disciples come to understand following Jesus's passion, crucifixion and resurrection is the nature of his kingship (see also Mark 10:45). It is still hidden from them, until they put the whole narrative together like a completed jigsaw, which then realigns their perspective, thinking and future vision. As with so much of Jesus's ministry and teaching, it is only truly grasped retrospectively, so radical is its presentation of kingship and Messianic calling.

Contrastingly, the Pharisees feel frustrated in their plans. Far from being able to arrest Jesus, they find that he is becoming increasingly popular as news of his raising of Lazarus spreads through the capital and amongst the incoming pilgrims (12:17–19). They cry out desperately, "look how the whole world has gone after him!" Nevertheless, as he enters the city on that first day of the Passover Week, Jesus knows *that his hour has come* and with it a more profound, revealing and eternal coronation.

The hour has come (12:20–36)

In many ways, this section is both the turning point and hinge of the Gospel. The section divides into three parts: the enquiry of the Greeks and the response of Jesus, the voice from heaven, and the urgency of the moment. In each context, Jesus stresses that the moment of his self-sacrifice for the world has come. Some Jewish Greeks, who are most probably pilgrims to the city, want to meet Jesus. They find Philip, who, while having a Greek name, is a Jew from Bethsaida in Galilee (1:44), and acts as an intermediary. Philip, together with Andrew, goes to Jesus and passes on the Greeks' request for an interview, but the time for leisurely interviews is over.

Jesus responds to the request for time with him by saying instead that "the hour has come for the Son of Man to be glorified" (12:23). This statement could very well be the title for this second part of the Gospel. "The hour" which had not come in the earlier part of the Gospel is now upon Jesus (see 2:4; 7:6). And it is time for the Son of Man to be glorified. We shall consider shortly the meaning of this glorification, but for now we can note that it involves life procured through sacrifice. Jesus compares his own glorification to a seed going into the ground and dying in order that it might produce more seeds. Only if the seed goes into the ground and, so to speak, dies, can more seed come. This is the pattern for the Son who will give up his life to obtain life for others. Indeed, it is the pattern for all servants of Christ who in giving up their lives for his sake will find life. In closing their fists around their own lives, they will find that even what they hold onto is taken away. This is well put by the martyred missionary Jim Elliot who said, "He is no fool who gives up what he cannot keep to gain what he cannot lose." Such a servant will be marked as a follower of Jesus and will be honoured by the Father.

At the same time, the reminder that the hour has come is deeply troubling. As in the Garden of Gethsemane when Jesus wrestled in prayer with the will of the Father (Matthew 26:36–46; Mark 14:32–42; Luke 22:39–46), so now he is troubled as he contemplates the near future and his death. His heart is troubled (Greek: *tetáraktai*), and during this internal struggle he asks the question, "What shall I say? 'Father save me from this hour?'" But it is a question to which he knows the answer deep down: "No", he responds, "it was for this very reason I came to this hour" (12:27b). Instead, he prays, "Father, glorify your name!"

The revelation of God's glory in the Incarnate Word is central to this Gospel. In the Prologue, John proclaims, "We have seen his glory, the glory of the One and Only, who came from the Father, full of grace and truth" (1:14). Again, after the first sign of turning the water into wine at Cana in Galilee, we are told, "he thus revealed his glory, and his disciples put their faith in him" (2:11). What then is the glory? In the Old Testament, the glory of God is shown to Israel at the giving of the Law, at the completion of the Temple, and in a vision such as Isaiah's in the year that King Uzziah dies (see Exodus 20:18; 33:12ff.; 1 Kings 8:10,11; Isaiah 6:1,2). It is sometimes described as the weight of his presence and is often mediated by a cloud or thick darkness disguising his majesty. Glory is commonly thought of today as being something splendid: a view of a magnificent building or scenery, a great occasion, or the full pomp of the monarchy at a royal occasion. In the context of these chapters, at the end of the Gospel, it is the revelation of the inner character of God himself, as displayed by Jesus in his sufferings on the cross. It is the revelation of mercy and justice, love and truth, humility and power, and forgiveness and holiness.

A bishop preparing an address in his study once took the gold cross from around his neck and laid it on his desk. A grandchild, aged six, came in and, seeing the cross, asked whether it was a key. About to say it was not, the bishop checked himself and said yes, it is a kind of key, perhaps recalling these words about the cross:

> It is the picture of violence
> Yet the key to peace
> It is a picture of suffering
> Yet the key to healing
> It is a picture of death
> Yet the key to life
> It is a picture of utter weakness
> Yet the key to power
> It is a picture of punishment
> Yet the key to mercy and forgiveness
> It is a picture of vicious hatred
> Yet the key to love
> It is a picture of complete humiliation
> Yet the Christian's supreme boast

Having prayed "glorify your name", Jesus hears a voice from heaven saying, "I have glorified it, and will glorify it again" (12:28). It is the Father speaking, as at the baptism and transfiguration of Jesus, recorded by the Synoptic Gospel writers (see Mark 1:11 and 9:2–13), reassuring Jesus that in what lies ahead the Father will glorify the Son: that is, he will reveal the true eternal character of God in the crucifixion and resurrection of Jesus in a powerful way. Jesus tells the listeners that the voice of the Father, which sounds like thunder, is for the benefit of the crowd and not for himself, so confident is he of the Father's love. Now, Jesus says, is *the moment* when, as he is lifted up on the cross, he will be able to draw all people to himself (12:32). The phrase "lifted up" not only shows the way he will die by being lifted up literally (Greek: *upsóō*) from the earth onto the wood of the cross, but also metaphorically. It means that Jesus will be exalted or glorified by the cross. What is intended as his humiliation and defeat will turn out to be victory and vindication (see 1 Corinthians 1:18ff.).

The crowd, who have seen his entrance into Jerusalem on a donkey and who have heard this teaching, are still struggling to get hold of who he is and what he is about to do (12:34). Jesus says that they are about to be overcome by darkness and that they should seek and put their trust in the light now (12:35–36). It is as if the opportunity that has been theirs for weeks and months is about to be snuffed out, much like a person snuffs out a candle in a dark place, allowing the darkness to spread. If they recognize the light, they should put their trust in it.

A final call (12:37–50)

It is not surprising that the closing section of this chapter should be given over to a final appeal by Jesus to the population to believe in him and the Father who has sent him (12:44). After all, these days provide the final opportunity for the earthly Jesus, the Word made flesh, to cry out to the people. Later, after the resurrection, it will be left to the Church (see 20:22,23). Despite all the miracles that Jesus has performed, many persist in their unbelief (12:37–40). Indeed, this had been prophesied by Isaiah, who said that God confirms them in the choice they have already made of not believing (12:40). The Gospel tells us that for an individual to gain eternal life, there must be the alignment of two factors: the giving of an individual by the Father to the Son in an action of overarching sovereignty (see 6:44), but also the movement of an individual's will to believe (see 7:37,38). Like stars in the solar system these two wills must come into alignment for the brightness of salvation to shine in a person's heart. The Pharisees, because caught up with the desire for praise from others, miss out. Likewise, others are intimidated by the fear of being put out of the synagogue and cannot believe. The fear of man overwhelms them.

Nevertheless, we are told, Jesus cries out (Greek *krádzō*, literally "shriek", "scream", "cry out").[60] What Jesus cries out is that to believe in him is to believe also in the one who sends him and to pass from darkness to light (12:46). Furthermore, those who reject Jesus's words will be judged by those very words, for they are not merely his words, but are given to him to speak by the Father (12:49). Thus, he knows what to say and, as importantly, how to say it (12:49b). Those words, if believed in, will bring eternal life (12:50).

So ends this important chapter of transition between Jesus's public ministry in Galilee and Jerusalem and the final days of more private ministry with the disciples before his most public death with the crowds, the High Priests, the Roman authorities and soldiers. The final week of Jesus's earthly life begins with his anointing for burial by Mary in Bethany, the triumphant procession into Jerusalem as the humble king, the acknowledgement that the hour has come, and the proclamation that his name will be glorified and his glory revealed. There is one last loud appeal to believe by Jesus himself before the week proceeds. John will now focus in the next five chapters on the teaching given to the disciples, by example and word, before the events of the Passion take hold.

---

60   Bauer, Arndt and Gingrich, *Greek Lexicon*, p. 448.

CHAPTER 14

A New Way and a New Commandment

John 13:1–38

If Chapter 12 is the transition from the public ministry of Jesus to his final teaching and passion, culminating in his crucifixion and resurrection, then the opening sentences of Chapter 13 are the summary of what is to come. In many ways, they are a new mini-prologue for what follows, and are thus worth quoting here:

> It was just before the Passover Feast. Jesus knew that the time had come for him to leave this world and go to the Father. Having loved his own who were in the world, he now showed them the full extent of his love.
>
> *John 13:1*

In several ways, these words parallel the Prologue. The time, rather than being "the beginning" (1:1), is now the Passover Feast, the most important Jewish festival recalling the liberation of Israel from slavery in Egypt. Jesus is now conscious, not of becoming the Incarnate Word (1:14), but rather of returning as the Incarnate Word to the side of the Father, bringing our humanity eternally to heaven. Throughout these final chapters of John there is a consciousness, not only of the exaltation of Jesus, but also that he is preparing his disciples for the future. Lastly, having already demonstrated his love in coming into the world, Jesus now shows the full extent of his love in sacrificing his life for theirs. What follows is a demonstration of the humility of Jesus in the foot-washing, the personification of the sin that mars our humanity in Judas, the weakness of our discipleship in Simon Peter's denial, and the call to a new way of living by following a New Commandment.

The foot-washing (13:2–17)

John introduces the foot-washing during the Last Supper with evident gravity and emphasis. At the same time, he is notably silent about the institution of the Lord's Supper or Eucharist itself, only referring later on in the narrative to a piece of bread being eaten (13:26). Knowing that the other Gospel writers have recorded the Last Supper, with its bread representing the body of Christ and its wine representing the blood, it seems John is content to say no more, especially as he records earlier Jesus's command to remember him and feed spiritually on his death in this way (see 6:53ff.). Instead, John focuses at this supper on what none of the other Gospel writers record, the washing of the disciples' feet. He very deliberately writes, "Jesus knew that the Father had put all things under his power, and that he had come from God and was returning to God; so, he got up from the meal, took off his outer clothing, and wrapped a towel round his waist. After that, he poured water into a basin and began to wash his disciples' feet, drying them with the towel that was wrapped round him" (13:3–5). These words speak more than anything of the humility of Jesus, his willingness to further divest himself of importance, to take on the role of a servant or slave, to do what was normally regarded as menial, and give his disciples an unforgettable example of leadership quite opposed to contemporary models of leading. In the narrative of the incarnation, which lies at the heart of this Gospel, the Word further casts self-regard aside as he serves those he has come to save.

There are two responses to Jesus's washing of the disciples' feet. The first is that of Simon Peter, who objects to Jesus washing his feet. I remember when leading a team on a visit to Malawi asking one of the two Africans on the team to pray for me. He found it difficult. He did not think that he had the right to pray for the leader. Of course, he had every right, but hitherto that had not been the model he had worked with. Peter does not feel comfortable with the Messiah and Son of God washing his feet! But Jesus says that unless he does so, Peter can have no part of this fellowship (13:8). On hearing this, Peter veers to the opposite extreme, saying, "not just my feet but my hands and my head as well!" (13:9).

The washing is both a menial act performed by Jesus for the disciples and a vivid example of service, but it is also a symbolic illustration of the need for cleansing from sin. Jesus makes the point in response to Peter's interjection that there is no need for Jesus to wash the whole person if he or she *has already had a bath* (13:10). Only the feet need washing. In the same way, those who have already believed have received forgiveness and a new status, or in the terms often used by Paul, they have been justified (see Romans 3:25,26). They only need that ongoing forgiveness, which is more like washing the feet.

Having answered Peter's objection and washed the disciples' feet, Jesus draws out the implications of what he has done. "Now that I, your lord and teacher, have washed your feet, you also should wash one another's feet. I have set you an example that you should do as I have done for you" (13:14,15). This washing of fellow disciples' feet is not simply an annual event to be performed only in the context of a liturgy on Maundy Thursday, good as that is. Rather, this attitude of humble service, giving no thought to self, was and is both to be a general disposition of every disciple and a reality in Christian fellowship and mission. I remember a colleague on a mission to Western Uganda, a former police inspector in the UK, going to speak in a prison in Hoima. African prisons are basic to say the least. Before he spoke, he washed many prisoners' feet. I imagine they never forgot it. He was following the example of Jesus.

The clothing of humility is vital in true Christian service. In one of his homilies on discipleship, Augustine of Hippo is reported to have said that the most important quality in Christian living is humility; the second most important is humility; and the third most important quality is humility. C. S. Lewis wrote that humility is not thinking less of yourself, but thinking of yourself less. And finally, the Apostle Paul asks the penetrating question, "What do you have that you did not receive? And if you did receive it, why do you boast as though you did not?" (1 Corinthians 4:7). There could be no more conclusive grounds for humility than that.

The act of betrayal (John 13:18–30)

The mood at the Last Supper apparently changes swiftly. If the washing
of the disciples' feet exhibits the nobility and surprising grace of Jesus,
now humans in the person of Judas exhibit by contrast the depths to
which we can sink. John has already given notice in the chapter that
as Jesus rises to put a towel around his waist to wash his disciples' feet,
the devil has already prompted Judas Iscariot, son of Simon, to betray
Jesus (13:2). It is a choice born out of greed, because the High Priests
are offering him 30 pieces of silver to betray Jesus to the temple guard.
He is to choose an unguarded moment when Jesus is out of the public
eye and hence more easily arrested. After the foot-washing, and using
a prophetic prediction from Psalm 41, Jesus makes it clear that a close
associate will betray the Messiah (13:18). For Jesus this is distressing. He
is troubled in his spirit and solemnly announces or bears witness to the
fact that he will be betrayed. It is at this point, and in the commotion this
accusation causes among the disciples, that the Beloved Disciple, John,
reclining next to Jesus, is commissioned by Simon Peter to ask which
disciple Jesus means (13:24). In a position of some intimacy, leaning
back against the breast of Jesus (Greek: *kólpos* in 13:23, "chest", and also
stēthos in 13:25, "chest" or "breast"), he asks him who he means. Jesus
replies indirectly, identifying the betrayer as the one to whom he gives a
piece of bread which has been dipped in the dish. The action of giving
this bread or sop (Greek: *psōmíon*), i.e., bread dipped in a mixture or
sauce, possibly of herbs (bitter?), is a sign of favour or a compliment to
another, and is used four times in this chapter and nowhere else in the
New Testament. As soon as Judas takes the sop, not only is he identified,
but he also yields more fully to Satan's leading. Jesus tells him to do what
he has to do quickly, a bit like the line in Macbeth's speech about the
murder of Duncan: "If it were done when t'is done, then twere well it
were done quickly" (Act 1, Scene VII). Yet this command to do whatever
is signified "quickly" evokes confusion among the disciples, who think
it refers either to buying food for the feast, perhaps only just begun, or
to giving something to the poor (13:29). What is clear is that as soon as
Judas leaves the room it is night. Once again darkness or night is used

to convey the evil or fear in humankind and also the presence of Satan's power (see also 1:5; 3:2; 3:19,20).

Darkness or night is a significant metaphor in the Gospel, beginning in the Prologue (1:4–5) and with Jesus claiming to be the Light of the World (8:12). He recognizes that a time will come when darkness will seem to rule and doing works of light will become harder. The spiritual darkness that follows when Judas goes out of the room—it probably being dark by then—reflects the great spiritual struggle that will ensue in which darkness appears to gain the upper hand. Come the resurrection, light will have been shown to triumph.

Old ways and new ways (13:31–38)

When Judas leaves and it is night, Jesus repeats the words first uttered when he knows his hour has come (12:23,28–29). The Son will glorify the Father, and the Father the Son. And this glorification spoken of earlier is the revelation of the inner majesty of God: his love and justice, his mercy and righteousness. The explanation of these almost mystical verses of mutual glorification of the Son by the Father and the Father by the Son underscores the unique insight of this Gospel concerning the reciprocity of the Trinity, into which the Spirit will shortly be drawn in Jesus's teaching. Although the text may be a little uncertain here, the meaning is still clear, for it has been part of the theme of the entire Gospel, namely that the Father, Son and Spirit work together. What one does all do, and what one is all are. The statement also presages the opening of the Upper Room discourse. Some commentators have suggested that Chapters 15 and 16 should be placed after 13:31, so that the words about departure (14:31) fall at the end of the whole section before the prayer in Gethsemane, which in John includes John 17. But there are difficulties with both settings.

There is a real sense in these verses that a final discourse of almost valedictory teaching is underway. "My children", Jesus says tenderly to his disciples, "I will be with you only a little longer." By this stage of the week, it could be that Jesus only has a few hours more with the disciples. This teaching is confined, it seems, to the hours before his arrest and after the Last Supper. And Jesus warns them, saying, "where I am going, you cannot come" (13:33). This enigmatic saying prompts another highly laden conversation, this time with Peter, which will forever mark him out, but not before Jesus lays down a new commandment for a new era.

The commandment famously is to "love one another. As I [Jesus] have loved you, so you must love one another" (13:34). It is a commandment for a new era. It is similar to the summary of the Law in the two great commandments (see Mark 12:29–31), but is given a new twist here, as it is specifically applied to the Christian community and the standard of love is "as Jesus has loved us". Although it appears to be followed in the early years, as Tertullian bears witness in his famous dictum, "See how these Christians love one another" (Tertullian, *Apologeticus* 37.9), sadly and tragically, differences in doctrinal opinion soon give way to the use of punishment, torture and death.

Rather than reacting to this new commandment, Peter is more intrigued by Jesus saying that he will not be long with them, and asks, "Lord, where are you going?" (13:36a). Sensing it will involve danger but not knowing of what sort, Peter then says: "Lord why can't I follow you now? I will lay down my life for you" (13:37). It is this categorical statement that draws from Jesus his fateful prediction, "I tell you the truth, before the cock crows, you will disown me three times!" (13:38).

It is part of the poignancy and reality of the chapter that the washing of the disciples' feet, with all its self-disregarding humility and call to a new standard of love, is set in the context of human weakness and failure: the betrayal of Judas, predicted but not forestalled, and the denial of Peter, which will form the background to the final great conversation of the Gospel (21:15–25). The contrast between divine love and human frailty could not be greater.

CHAPTER 15

The Trinity Revealed

John 14:1–31

If evidence is needed of the Trinitarian nature of this Gospel and, more importantly, of the Trinitarian nature of God, then John 14 provides it. Each member of the Triune God is unveiled here, as is their relationship to each other. In no other Gospel is this explained, and even in the Epistles there is no such personal and authoritative explanation of the coexistence of Father, Son and Spirit as the one given here by Jesus himself. Thus, it is the Gospel of the sending Father, the Incarnate Son and the life-giving Spirit. What becomes clear is that to know one is to know all.

Jesus begins by consoling his disciples with further knowledge of the future. He has already tantalizingly said on several occasions that his days on earth with them are numbered (13:33). Indeed, he tells the crowd as much some months earlier (see 8:21) when he says he will go somewhere unbelieving Jews cannot come. Jesus is more comforting to his own disciples here, however. He tells them not to be troubled at the news of his going, but rather to trust him and the Father who sent him (14:1).

The grounds for such trust are that in his Father's house there are many rooms (Greek: *pollaí monaí*, "many abodes" or "dwellings") and he, Jesus, is going ahead to prepare a resting place there for each of them. Furthermore, not knowing the time of his return by his own admission (see Mark 13:32), which is something known only to the Father, Jesus thinks that he will return soon to take or escort them to these heavenly quarters. Thomas then typically has the honesty to say, "Lord, we don't know where you are going, so how can we know the way?" (14:5). Saying this, he elicits from Jesus one of the most revealing statements about

Jesus's relationship and access to the Father, and one of the great (the last or seventh) "I am" sayings of the Gospel. Jesus tells Thomas, and all who will listen, "I am the way and the truth and the life. No one comes to the Father except through me" (14:6). He then goes further in describing his relationship with the Father than he has ever done before, saying, "If you really knew me, you would know my Father" (14:7).

The key word here, as so often with John's writings and indeed Jesus's teaching, is *knowing* (Greek: *ginōskō*, "to know"). The word takes us, as we might expect, back to the Prologue, where this great theme is first laid out. There John tells us, "No one has ever seen God, but God the One and Only, who is at the Father's side, has *made him known*" (1:18). What Jesus is saying in the Upper Room is that the disciples will be entering into a deeper level of knowledge through the coming week, involving as it will his passion, crucifixion and resurrection. And in properly understanding these things, as they eventually will, they will gain a deeper knowledge of the Father and Son, and, as we shall see, of the Spirit. For these reasons Jesus can confidently say, "From now on you do know him [the Father] and have seen him" (14:7b).

At this point, Philip, not yet understanding, asks one more question. Perhaps it is the question others dare not utter for fear of seeming spiritually obtuse. He says, "show us the Father and that will be enough (or "we will be satisfied")" (14:8). Jesus's reply seems almost to reflect exasperation or, if not, amazement at their lack of understanding. In fairness, it is a large matter to understand, and it would take the Church almost three centuries to formally do so in the Nicene Creed of AD 325. In what must be one of the most revealing statements of the Gospel, Jesus says:

> Don't you know me, Philip, even after I have been among you such a long time? Anyone who has seen me has seen the Father. ... Don't you believe that I am in the Father, and the Father is in me? The words I say to you are not just my own. Rather, it is the Father, living in me, who is doing his work. Believe me when I say that I am in the Father and the Father is in me; or at least believe on the evidence of the miracles themselves.
>
> *John 14:9–11*

In a few sentences, Jesus explains that there is complete mutual indwelling between the Father and the Son, as he has already said in John 10:30: "I and the Father are one." This unity of being, or as the early Church agrees to describe it, this unity of *substance* (Greek: *ousia*) lies at the heart of the Godhead. This is not to say that each member of the Godhead does not also have a distinct role, but rather that each shares in the work and substance of the others. In trying to express this unity and distinctiveness of the Godhead, one of the Church Fathers, Gregory of Nyssa from Cappadocia, put it like this:

> All that the Father is, we see revealed in the Son; all that the Son is the Father is also; for the whole Son dwells in the Father, and has the whole Father dwelling in himself. The Son who exists always in the Father can never be separated from him, nor can the Spirit be divided from the Son who through the Spirit works all things. He who receives the Father also receives at the same time the Son and the Spirit.[61]

The significance of this is that Jesus is more than an inspired man, more than a memorable teacher, or indeed a miracle-worker. He is what John says from the very start of the Gospel: God in the flesh (1:14). And because of the indwelling of the Father in the Son, Jesus's words and actions are equally revelatory of God's ways and truth.

Furthermore, believing in Jesus has great consequences for his disciples, and in particular the Apostles, whom he is addressing here. The first point is that when Jesus returns to the Father, his disciples, empowered by the Spirit, will be able to perform greater works, not *in quality*, but *in quantity*, because they will eventually be scattered across the world. One of the reasons for this will be prayer. Where prayer is offered in Jesus's name, that is according to his purpose and character, and where it glorifies the Father, then it will have a ready response; indeed, Jesus will do it. Where a prayer offered in his name, and with the desire of glorifying the Father, does not appear to get a positive answer,

---

[61]   St Gregory of Nyssa, *Letters*, "Letter 38 to Basil", tr. J Deferrari, Loeb Classical Series (Boston, MA: Harvard University Press, 1926), p. 226.

then the best way forward is, in the words of an African proverb, "to pray until something happens" (PUSH). The prayer will be answered, although not necessarily in the way we thought. But remember, too, that further help is offered, to which point we now move.

The Coming of the Spirit (14:15–31)

Teaching about the Spirit is intermittent but ongoing throughout the Gospel. It is true that, unlike in Luke, we don't have an account of the Spirit's work in the incarnation itself, as in the story of Mary's conception of Jesus the Messiah, and in the various promptings of the main characters around the nativity. John nevertheless speaks tantalizingly of the Spirit's presence and work: telling us that Jesus will baptize in the Spirit, as he was himself immersed in the Spirit at his own baptism (1:32,33); that to be born all over again requires the work of the Spirit (3:5ff.); and that it is the Spirit who will flow from us like streams of living water if we come to Christ and drink (7:38,39). What has been hinted at through the Gospel is now explained more fully than in any other Gospel, in particular the relationship of the Spirit to the Father and the Son. In other words, the nature of the Trinity and the relationships between its members are highlighted in a way that does not occur elsewhere in Scripture, and more than that, the disciples or the members of the Church are to be folded into, or incorporated in, this relationship.

First, Jesus makes it clear that love for the Son is demonstrated by following his commandments. This will be a consistent theme through this teaching in the Upper Room (see also 15:10). Inevitably, there is a moral dimension to discipleship, which elsewhere has been summarized as loving God and loving neighbour (see Mark 12:29–31). This means fulfilling the commandments, and the only way of doing so is through love, for love is the fulfilling of the Law (Romans 13:8–10; Galatians 5:14). If, on the one hand, we set ourselves to fulfil the Law and so demonstrate our love for Christ, he in turn will ask the Father, and the Father "will give you another Counsellor to be with you for ever—the Spirit of Truth" (14:16,17). That the Spirit is a Spirit of truth is consistent with the entire emphasis on truth in the Gospel. This truth is about God, ourselves and our own integrity. The Spirit is not known to "the world", that is, to the human community which does not believe in God. Left to itself that community can neither "see him" nor "know him", but the disciples already know him through the presence of Jesus, and soon he will be "in them".

Hence, a defining characteristic of a Christian will be the indwelling of the Spirit (14:17). For this reason, the disciples will not be orphans when Jesus returns to the Father; instead, the Spirit will indwell them. Furthermore, "on that day", which is either the day of resurrection or Pentecost or both, the disciples will come to a remarkable revelation that "I am in my Father, and you are in me and I am in you." This reciprocal indwelling both within and amongst the Trinity and in the disciples is surely one of the great revelations of this Gospel. Paul will further explicate this in Romans 8, but no other Gospel writer does.

The Church Fathers, and particularly the Cappadocians, had a term for this: *perichoresis*, which literally means a rotation or a dance of the persons of the Trinity, among and between them. This "dance" is later to incorporate the disciples. This surely also lies behind the Eastern Orthodox theology of *theosis*, which holds that God's intention is to make us like God himself. This too is behind Athanasius's famous dictum: "He became man that we might become divine; and he revealed himself through a body that we might receive an idea of the invisible Father; and he endured insults from men that we might inherit incorruption."[62] Once again Jesus says that proof of loving him is keeping the commandments, and the one who demonstrates this love "will be loved by my Father, and I too will love him and show myself to him" (14:21). This surely has been the experience of the saints down the ages. The anchorite or hermit Julian of Norwich had an extraordinary experience of God's presence and love when very ill and whilst in her cell (still visible in Norwich) in the fourteenth century. When she enquired of God what this experience meant, she wrote:

---

[62]   Athanasius, *De incarnatione*, tr. Robert W. Thomson (Oxford: Oxford University Press, 1971), p. 269.

And fifteen years and more later my spiritual understanding received an answer, which was this: Do you want to know what your Lord meant? Know well that love was what he meant. Who showed you this? Love. What did he show? Love. Why did he show it to you? For love. Hold fast to this and you will know and understand more of the same; but you will never understand or know from it anything else for all eternity. This is how I was taught that our Lord's meaning was love.[63]

After questions from Thomas (14:5) and Philip (14:8), there follows the third question of this chapter, this time from the little-known disciple Judas, the son of James (see Luke 6:16). He asks, "But Lord, why do you intend to show yourself to us and not to the world?" (14:22). Jesus's answer to this question is not exactly direct and seems mostly recapitulation of what he has already told them.

He reiterates that love for Jesus must demonstrate itself in obedience, for, "If anyone loves me, he will obey my teaching." Then the Father and Son, presumably by the Spirit, will come and "make [their] home" with a disciple (14:23). The Spirit, whom he again calls the Counsellor (as earlier in 14:16), will remind them of all that he has said. The term "Counsellor" is a translation of the Greek word *parákleton* or "paraclete", meaning literally "the one who draws alongside". He will be sent by the Father in the name of Jesus, a Trinitarian combination if ever there was one. Drawing a distinction between the world and the life of God, Jesus then says that the peace he gives will be beyond anything the world gives. It will not just be the cessation of hostility or animosity, but a profound peace that gives health at the deepest level to the individual. There is no need for fear or anxiety (14:27).

Finally, Jesus reiterates that time is short. The hour is very nearly upon him. Darkness is about to be brought by the prince of this world (14:30). Yet this prince has no power over Jesus, who will return to be with the Father as the pre-incarnate Word but now embodying in heaven true humanity and divinity. This should be cause for rejoicing for the

---

[63]   Julian of Norwich, *Revelations of Divine Love*, tr. Elizabeth Spearing (Harmondsworth: Penguin Classics, 1998).

disciples, as it marks the completion of the Son's work on earth. It also marks the restoration of the heavenly rule of Father, Son and Spirit, and it further demonstrates that the Son's love for the Father is uniquely shown by exact and complete obedience (14:28–31).

If this chapter of John's Gospel has shown supremely the relationship between Father, Son and Spirit, the next three chapters, preceding the events of the Passion and the crucifixion, will show what Jesus intends for the disciples, and how they are to be enfolded into this Trinitarian fellowship whilst on earth, teaching that is both profoundly hopeful and consoling.

CHAPTER 16

The True Vine

John 15:1–27

John 14 reveals the nature of the Trinity by showing that each member is distinct but shares a common Godhead. John 15 dramatically shows through a time-honoured allegory that now the Church is to be included in this fellowship and mission of the Triune God. Paul puts it in different terms in Ephesians 3:10–12, but with the same underlying meaning. Indwelling the Church is the way in which God manifests himself to the world and the universe into eternity. Whatever we may think of the Church, with its multiple wrinkles and blemishes, this is its long-term destination.

In the narrative in John, there is a break at the end of Chapter 14, where Jesus says, "Come now, let us leave" (14:31). With these words he and the disciples leave the Upper Room and walk through dark streets to the Temple Court, where "in front of them, glinting in the light of the full moon, was the Golden Vine that trailed over the Temple porch".[64] This image of the vine, so often used of Israel in the Old Testament (see Psalm 80:8–19; Isaiah 5:1–7), is the cue for Jesus's next teaching, which is among the most profound in the Gospel. Israel is the vine, but it is to be expanded and fulfilled to include the Gentiles. Now all disciples are like branches on the vine of which Jesus is himself the root or stock. His Father is the vinedresser (Greek: *geōrgós*, from which we get "George", meaning "farmer", "earth worker" or "gardener"). The Father does the

---

[64] William Temple, *Readings in St John's Gospel* (London: Macmillan, 1949), p. 250.

work of the vinedresser: cutting away dead wood, pruning and clearing, or in this case cleaning by the words of *the Word* (see 15:2–4).

The job of the branch or the disciple is to abide or remain in the vine. Fruitfulness is dependent on abiding or remaining (Greek: *ménō*, "to remain", "stay" or "dwell"). So long as the branch remains in the vine, with the periodic pruning that will come with that, it will go on bearing fruit. The secret of fruitfulness is to remain or abide in the vine, for "apart from me you can do nothing" (15:5). I remember reading those verses with another very soon after becoming a disciple. They struck me forcibly and also underlined my own dependence. Ever since then, and and especially since ordination in 1976, I have uttered those words as a prayer before undertaking any form of ministry.

Remaining or abiding must mean prayerful dependence, being continually cleansed by the Word, and being fed by the sap of the vine. The branch that does not remain in the stem or stock of the vine will become unfruitful and may be removed. Jesus gives this warning so that this may not happen to us, and that we may remain (15:6). Conversely, the branch that remains and keeps drawing the sap from the vine will become fruitful and this fruit will abide. An aid to fruitfulness is prayer, and prayers which result from such remaining or abiding in which the word or teaching of Jesus also dwells in the heart of a believer will be answered. This does not mean that they will be answered in the way we suppose, or indeed want, but they will be heard and answered and glory will be given to the Father (15:7,8).

Remaining in God's love (John 15:9–17)

The next section of this allegory develops the theme, using the same idea of remaining, but deepening its meaning. Jesus adds that to abide or remain in him, the vine, is in fact to remain in his love in the same way that he himself abides or remains in the Father's love. Once again there is more than a note of reciprocity here and also a widening circle of meaning. To remain in Jesus's love is to obey his commandments, just as Jesus always obeys his Father's commands and thus remains in his love (see 14:31 and 15:10). The result of such loving obedience will be joy (15:11). A parallel can be found in human relations in which love for another is shown in wanting to please them and fulfil their wishes (assuming that they are good), with the result for both parties being joy and a reciprocal desire to please. The command that Jesus particularly draws our attention to, and which he has just given to this new community of the Church, is "love each other as I have loved you" (13:34,35; 15:12). Jesus shows the extent of this love in his case for the Church and in our case for each other. Such love may even involve the laying down of our lives. It is in this context that Jesus gives the peerless words and concept of sacrificial service, saying, "Greater love has no one than this, that they lay down their life for their friends" (15:13).

It is at this point that Jesus introduces a new term for a disciple, now no longer described in terms of the allegory, that is, as a branch remaining in the vine, but as a friend (Greek: *phílos*, "friend"). Once again friendship with Jesus depends on doing what he commands, and especially the commandment to love one another. Furthermore, and once again in typical Johannine style, the point deepens like a spiritual corkscrew going further with every turn. His followers are friends rather than servants, because the basis of this friendship is knowing the "business" or simply the doings of the Son (15:15). Again, the reciprocal nature of this teaching is evident: the Son has treated us in the same way as he has been treated by the Father. So, it is made plain that "everything that I learned from my Father I have made known to you" (15:15b).

Finally in this section, and before a rather sobering change of tack after these many comforting spiritual insights, Jesus tells his disciples that at the root of his friendship and relationship is the choice that *he made* in choosing his disciples to go and bear fruit (15:16). Again in the Gospel, and as we have seen often enough, our own spiritual response is enabled by a previous action between the Father and the Son (see especially 6:37 and 44). In this instance our fruitfulness is traced back to his initial choice of us, a calling that includes the basic vocation to go and bear fruit. Prayer (see also 15:7; 14:13,14) is the means whereby we may be fruitful (15:16b). Before turning to the difficulties that can be expected, Jesus reiterates for the third time in this discourse (see 13:34,35; 15:12) that his disciples are to "love each other" (15:17).

Trouble ahead (15:18–16:4)

The final part of Chapter 15 and the early verses of Chapter 16 deal with the persecution that awaits the Apostles and the Church. Once again there is a note of reciprocity about this teaching: what happened to Jesus will happen to the Church. The spiritual struggle is the same (see Paul's explanation in Ephesians 6:12ff.). Jesus begins with the warning that "if the world hates you, keep in mind that it hated me first" (15:18). Here "world" means a society that is devoted to its own interests and not to the glory of God. Furthermore, such is the nature of the world that it loves its own and hates those who do not share its implicit assumptions and join in its actions (15:19). This will prove utterly true of the Church in Roman society, such that when its members cannot accept the militaristic values of the empire, or will not take part in its pagan worship, or go to games in the amphitheatres where bloodlust is so evident, or when they prize sexual purity; then they are despised, indeed harried by the populace as well as by the magistracy. In a word, they are hated; and they cannot be too quickly punished or made a spectacle of. All this is coming to the disciples in the future, just as it will come to Jesus very soon (15:20). The same treatment will be given to the servant as is given to the master (15:20).

Jesus goes on to explain that the very words and works he has spoken and done will provoke hostility. The reason for this is perverse. If Jesus's opponents allow these words and works to lead them to the conclusion that he is sent by the Father, and indeed is one with the Father (15:22–24), then they will have to surrender their independence and authority to him. However wise his words and however powerful his deeds, that is the one thing they cannot and will not do. Instead, they deny the reality of his words and deeds and punish their author. This only increases their guilt, Jesus says (15:22). And if they do this to him, they will do the same to others who bear his name, as indeed they do in Jerusalem straight after Pentecost when the Apostles and other disciples, such as Stephen, are hauled before the Sanhedrin repeatedly and sometimes punished (see Acts 4:5ff.; 5:17; 7:1ff.).

Jesus once more warns the disciples of what lies ahead so that they "will not go astray" (16:1). The Apostles will face being put out of the synagogue. Moreover, Jesus is flagging up a coming division between the Church and the Jewish community as formed in the synagogue. Not only will they be ostracized by the synagogue in the future for preaching and maintaining that Jesus is the Messiah and the Son of God, but they will also be in danger of losing their lives; with the authorities seeing such punishment as performance of a religious service (16:2). The Jews will see it as a defence of Judaism and Moses, and the Roman authorities will see it as a defence of their pagan gods. They will do these things because they cannot grasp the relationship between the Father and the Son (16:3). Jesus wants his followers to be fully in the know, so that forewarned, they will be forearmed (16:4).

Once again, and in the midst of this teaching, Jesus assures the disciples they will not be alone. The Counsellor, whom the Son will request of the Father, the Spirit of Truth, will support them in their testimony that the Son really is the Incarnate Word of God, the Messiah and Son of God (15:26–27). Of the Spirit and of impending events, Jesus now has much more to say.

CHAPTER 17

Assistance at Hand: Joy Awaits

John 16:1–33

Jesus continues his preparation of the disciples for the future, which in itself is very instructive, since so much of our lives revolve around leaving and beginning. This may mean leaving school and beginning a job, leaving university and starting a profession, relocating to a new country or position, leaving a parental home for marriage, adapting to demanding children, facing retirement after busy years of service, or dealing with loss of one kind or another, whether it is an empty nest, the loss of a partner, or even a child. As usual Shakespeare puts it well, saying all men and women "have their exits and their entrances".[65] All these progressions require change and new challenges. In the Bible, there are several critical moments of new departures for Israel: the death of Moses and entry into the Promised Land, the experience of exile by the waters of Babylon (Psalm 137 and Ezekiel 1), and the return of the exiles to the broken-down walls and the desecrated Temple of Jerusalem. These are endings and new beginnings.

And now Jesus, who has repeatedly promised that he will leave the disciples, says that the hour for his departure has come. Although there have been half-hearted enquiries as to his destination, none have asked what awaits him (16:5). Peter's earlier enquiry (13:36) has been lost in his own protestations of loyalty. Nevertheless, Jesus recognizes that the disciples are preoccupied with their own sense of loss and grief, and it is this he now addresses. Firstly, he tells them of the assistance that is to come.

---

[65] Shakespeare, *As You Like It, The Seven Ages of Man*, Act II, Scene 7.

The assistance of the Spirit (16:7–16)

Once again Jesus talks about the work of the Spirit whom they are still to receive (see 7:39 and 20:22). Again, he calls the Spirit the Comforter (Greek: *paráklētos*, "the one who comes alongside"). Jesus explains that his departure is to their advantage, since as a man he can only be in one place at one time, whereas the Spirit can be in all his people and in all places. The gift of the Spirit is inestimable. Indeed, Cyril of Jerusalem, a fourth-century theologian, wrote these words in one of his Catechetical Lectures preparing candidates for baptism: "The Spirit comes gently and makes himself known by his fragrance. He is not felt as burden, for God is light, very light. Rays of light and knowledge stream from before him as the Spirit approaches. The Spirit comes with the tenderness of a true friend to save, to heal, to teach, to counsel, to strengthen and to console."[66]

Jesus goes on to describe another way in which the activity of the Spirit will assist. He will not only work in the Church, and in the hearts and lives of the disciples, but in the world outside the Church as well. The Spirit will have a reproving or prosecuting role also. Indeed, the Greek word chosen here is *elégchō*, meaning to bring to light, expose, set forth or convince someone of something. He will convict, that is, give an internal and powerful witness with regard to sin, righteousness, and judgement. In other words, he will help the unbelieving world draw the right and convicting conclusion about the reality of sin, the true standard of righteousness, and the necessity of judgement. Jesus elaborates by saying he will convict the sinner of not believing, and of not understanding the standard of righteousness he embodies, and of the necessity of judgement because of the evil that patently exists in the world and human history. Surely it was the first of these three convictions that left C. S. Lewis on his knees in Magdalen College in the Trinity Term of 1929:

> You must picture me alone in that room, feeling, whenever my mind lifted even for a second from my work, the steady unrelenting approach of him whom I so earnestly desired not to

---

[66] Cyril, *Catechetical Lecture* XVII §11ff., NAPNF Second Series, Vol. VII (Cosimo, 2007), p. 127.

meet. That which I greatly feared had at last come upon me. In the Trinity Term of 1929, I gave in and admitted God was God, and knelt and prayed: perhaps that night, the most dejected and reluctant convert in all England. I did not then see what is now the most shining and obvious thing, the Divine humility which will accept a convert on his own feet. The Prodigal Son at least walked home on his own feet. But who can truly adore that Love which will open the high gates to a Prodigal son who is brought in kicking, struggling, resentful, and darting his eyes in every direction for a chance of escape?[67]

Surely it was the Spirit who prompted Lewis with his convicting and convincing power? In effect, in the above sentences, Jesus promises that the Spirit requested by him and sent by the Father (16:7) will assist them in their mission. It will not be up to them to convince their hearers, but the Spirit will assist in this action of conviction, thus turning men, women and children to Jesus in faith. This assistance will go further: Jesus recognizes that the disciples cannot take any more in, so like a good teacher, he promises that the Spirit in the future will guide them "into all truth" (16:12,13), speaking not on his own authority, divine though he is, but on the authority of the Son and the Father. Once again this underlines the Trinitarian point that what one member of the Trinity does, all do (16:13b). This action by the Spirit will bring glory to the Son, "by taking from what is mine and making it known to you" (16:14). This knowledge in turn belongs to the Father and comes from the Father to the Son (16:15). Thus, just as the Spirit brings the presence of the Father and the Son to the disciple (14:23), so he also brings truth, and, Jesus says, knowledge of the future also. For "he", the Spirit, "will tell you what is to come" (16:13c). In all these ways, the Spirit will assist in the mission of the Church and in its teaching and life, and is hence of inestimable value.

At this point, Jesus changes the direction of the conversation. Indeed, throughout this teaching in the Upper Room and in the Temple Courts, Jesus intermingles teaching about the future, as well as teaching about the action of Father, Son and Spirit in the lives of the disciples, with vivid

---

[67]   C. S. Lewis, *Surprised by Joy* (London: Fontana Collins, 1955), p. 182.

reminders that he is in the last hours of his earthly life, with its greatest climax ahead, and indeed the fulfilment of the purpose for which he came. For now, the Son of Man must be glorified (12:23). Jesus then mysteriously says, "in a little while you will see me no more, and then after a little while you will see me" (16:16). Not surprisingly, this statement provokes many questions among the disciples about its meaning. "In a little while you will see me no more but after a little while you will see me" sounds like a contradiction until we realize that he is speaking about his death by crucifixion and his inextinguishable life by resurrection. Jesus now goes about explaining his meaning with an illustration.

The joy of new birth (16:19–28)

Jesus recognizes the questions in the disciples' minds without them directly asking him. He says: "Are you asking one another what I meant when I said, 'In a little while you will see me no more, and then after a little while you will see me'?" (16:19). He explains that in the coming days they will go through a roller coaster of emotions, not unlike a woman giving birth. Firstly, around the time of his passion and crucifixion, they will experience great grief: not only at their own loss of his presence, but also over his pain and dereliction during the crucifixion. Furthermore, they will be distressed by their own desertion of Jesus in his great hour of need (16:32). All this will cause them great grief, not unlike the pain a woman goes through in labour when giving birth to a child. But at dawn, light and hope will come: "You will grieve", says Jesus, "but your grief will turn to joy" (16:20b). Like a woman who has given birth, the pain will be forgotten (mostly) in the delight of a child safely born; and great joy will replace grief and distress (16:21,22). Likewise, the disciples' joy at the resurrection, and in particular at seeing Jesus again, will replace their grief at the crucifixion. Once again, it is teaching full of realism and hope, explaining and anticipating the emotions that the disciples will go through in the coming days, and elucidating, in graphic terms, those earlier words about being seen no more and then seen again.

Nor is this all. Jesus says that when they see him again, they will have new confidence and greater incentive to pray. When Jesus returns to the Father the disciples will learn to pray to the Father in a way they have not done before. Previously, they have literally asked Jesus both for explanations and also for their own needs to be met. Now they are to approach the Father in the name or character of Jesus, making their requests in prayer. If they ask, they will receive, and their joy will be full (16:23,24). This will be a further benefit to them, and will only increase their joy. They can approach the Father with confidence in this way, because as they have loved Jesus, they have also been loved, and are loved, by the Father (16:27). One could summarize this by saying that Jesus's mission is to restore fellowship between humanity and the Father by his work, and to enable humankind to approach the Father in confidence, love and hope (see Ephesians 2:14–22 and 3:12 where, not surprisingly, Paul comes to the same conclusion as John).

Jesus is now focused on his return to the Father from whence he came and on what this means for the disciples. Throughout the Gospel, from the Prologue onwards, there has been this emphasis that, as the eternal pre-existent Word, Jesus has come from the Father, is sent by him to the world to bring salvation, and will then return to the Father in triumph, having completed his work (see 1:18; 5:36–38; 16:28). This moment is nearly at hand. Later, after his resurrection, Jesus will no longer speak figuratively (see 16:25), but will teach plainly that the Messiah was always intended to suffer and to rise again, that he might redeem Israel and the Gentiles. Luke, who records these post-resurrection conversations, makes this particularly clear (see Luke 24:17–27 and Acts 1:3). Having died and risen again, Jesus will abandon figurative teaching about these things, and in a plain manner explain from the Scriptures why these things were always planned and intended from eternity (see also 1 Peter 1:17–20).

Now we understand (16:29–33)

At the end of the chapter and after Jesus's teaching, the disciples in effect say, "now we understand." But as anyone knows who has been following Christ for a while, there are layers upon layers of understanding. It would be fair to say that the disciples *think they understand* but in fact have some way to go. Often showing themselves obtuse, it is not until well after the resurrection that they understand what it was all about. After all, only minutes ago in the Upper Room Philip has said, "Show us the Father, and that will be enough for us" (14:8). But here they are, effusive in their declarations, almost as if they have veered from one extreme to another in their perceptions (16:30). Perhaps glibly, they say, "This makes us believe that you came from God" (16:30). As early as in the first chapter, Nathanael has said, "Rabbi, you are the Son of God: you are the King of Israel" (1:49), which he says because of Jesus's knowledge of his whereabouts under the fig tree earlier in the day (1:48). Although Andrew and Peter appear to have also understood Jesus to be the Messiah at that point (see 1:41), one wonders if their belief was more like a weathervane than an anchor. It seems that confidence in the identity of Jesus waxes and wanes in the minds of the disciples. But here they appear convinced: "This [teaching] makes us believe that you came from God" (16:30).

Jesus replies with astonishment mixed with irony, "You believe at last!", implying they have left it to the last moment, or "what more would it take?" Nevertheless, despite their protestation of belief and loyalty, Jesus says they will be scattered (16:32), or one might say more harshly, they will all desert him, except for John, who remains at the cross with Mary (19:25–27). Jesus then says, "And me you leave alone" (Greek: *kàmé mónon aphēte*, literally "me alone you leave"). It is a desolate moment after three years of almost constant care of the disciples. Jesus quickly adds that he will not be entirely alone (until those hours of complete abandonment on the cross), as his Father is with him (16:32). It is a personal revelation rare in the Gospels, which the Beloved Disciple records, showing the cost to Jesus of his exacting path. Despite this, Jesus raises his own and his disciples' spirits with the resounding statement, "I have said this to you, that in me you may have peace. In the world you have tribulation; but be of good cheer; I have overcome the world" (16:33). Unfortunately, there can be tribulation in the Church also! (Greek: *thlīpsis*, meaning "pressure", "affliction", "oppression" and "tribulation", and see also Romans 5:3). The promise is nevertheless that in Jesus peace may be found (Greek: *eirēne*, "peace"). Peace is one of the great gifts of Jesus, as demonstrated by this Gospel (see 14:27). And now in further self-giving love for the Church, Jesus turns to prayer.

CHAPTER 18

Jesus's Prayer for the Church

John 17:1–26

The five chapters from John 13 to 17 are all about the preparation of the disciples for the future. So far this has included an example of humble service in the washing of the disciples' feet; forewarning of impending events which will involve the betrayal by one disciple and the denial by another; the giving of a new commandment to love one another as Jesus has loved them; the revelation of the full panoply of the Trinity and its activity, and in particular the gift of the Holy Spirit; the call to be fruitful by abiding in Christ, and the Father and Spirit making their home in their hearts: the forewarning of trials and persecution ahead; and finally, the promise of further assistance from the Spirit, as well as joy and peace. Nor is that everything. It seems that at some point before crossing the Kidron Valley, quite possibly through Solomon's Colonnade and the Shushan Gate on the Temple Mount, and entering Gethsemane, which has a garden of olive trees (18:1), Jesus prays for the disciples and the future of the Church. It seems that while he is standing in the Temple precincts with his disciples, they overhear his prayer for them and for the future of the Church.

Before looking at the three-part prayer itself—for Jesus himself, for the disciples, and for those who will believe through the disciples, i.e., the future Church—we must underline the significance of prayer. It is true that in John's Gospel there are fewer occasions recorded when Jesus leaves the disciples to go off and pray alone (see Mark 1:35; Luke 6:12; Matthew 14:13), although, as in the Synoptic Gospels, John does record him slipping away from the crowds after the Feeding of the Five Thousand to avoid being press-ganged into their vision of kingship (see

John 6:15). But uniquely here John records verbatim the prayer he hears Jesus pray in the Temple precincts before adjourning to Gethsemane.

Once again it is the Synoptic Gospels which record Jesus's Gethsemane prayer. What we can glean from John's account, however, is that no preparation of the disciples is complete without the prayer of Jesus to his Father. It is the final way of preparing the disciples spiritually for what lies ahead and is in itself a powerful illustration of how teaching and example must still be accompanied by prayer for the complete equipping of an effective disciple. In other words, it is not enough just telling the disciples what is true, or showing them how to act, unless this is accompanied by prayer. Prayer allows the seed of the Word to permeate the soul, it clears a spiritual path for action, and it equips the disciple, and hence the Church, with the authority of God. It is the slender nerve that moves the hand of God.

Jesus prays for his final hours (17:1–5)

Jesus begins the prayer with at least two requests. In a typically Johannine way, Jesus recognizes that the hour has now finally come: the hour of his passion, the hour of the cross and the resurrection. He prays twice in this short prayer that he will be "glorified", a request we thought about in Chapter 12. Once again, this glorification will be reciprocal: the Son being glorified will mean glory for the Father as well. And this glorification will be a completing of the glory that Jesus has already brought to the Father through his words and actions. A further special insight is given in the repetition of this request in verse five, where Jesus says, "And now, Father, glorify me in your presence [meaning before him in the world and whilst on the cross] with the glory I had with you before the world began" (17:5). Here is a clear indication in Jesus's own words of his pre-existent life before the incarnation; indeed "before the world began" (17:5).

The second request is that the eternal life which Jesus has been commissioned to give will be given to all those "you have given him" (17:2). Once again in John's Gospel, there is a strong sense that those who believe in Jesus are a gift from the Father to the Son (6:37). They are to have *eternal life*, which is simply, profoundly and wonderfully described as *knowing God*, the only true God, and Jesus Christ, who God has sent (17:3). Having prayed for this gift of eternal life to be given to all those given to him by the Father, and for his own glorification in the events of his passion, crucifixion and resurrection, Jesus moves on to pray very intentionally for his own disciples.

Jesus prays for his disciples (17:6–19)

What Jesus prays for his disciples can be summarized as two main ideas: they are to be set apart by the words that Jesus speaks to them, and then protected (Greek: *tēreō*, "keep from harm", "watch over", "guard") in their witness to the Son in the future. Both these ideas, which take centre stage in Jesus's prayer, need to be explored further, as both are also bound up with the actions of Jesus.

At the beginning of this part of the prayer, Jesus affirms that these disciples are in the first place a gift from the Father: "You gave them to me and they have obeyed your word" (17:6). He has given them the Father's words in his ministry (17:8). Furthermore, the disciples have come to understand that this teaching, or the words spoken by Jesus, come from the Father originally (see 12:49 also). Receiving and understanding the words of Jesus has the effect of setting the disciples apart for a mission in the world. Jesus says the effect is that the world hates them (17:14), and here "hate" has the peculiar Jewish sense of preferring one's own kind to the priorities and outlook of the disciples. In effect, the disciples will easily become social outcasts: thrown out of the synagogues (see 15:18ff.), despised for believing that a crucified man could be the Messiah, and ridiculed for believing that their master rose from the dead. Nevertheless, Jesus prays that God's will may be sanctified in the truth of his words and teaching and that, as such, the disciples are to be sent out into the world. They are not to be taken out of the world (17:15), but are instead to be sent into it (17:18).

This surely is the history of the Church in mission, when at its best— on the one hand holding on to the transforming effect of the Word, or on the other, being received with either great hostility or joy. We need only think of the reception of the Church in the Muslim world today, in countries such as Iran, to see that there is great hostility towards Christians, while equally there is great joy among many in the same country who believe. Indeed, there appears to have been an upsurge of Christianity there, and of Iranian Christians in England. Equally, there is a large minority of Christians in China, despite the government's suffocating measures against the Church. What is clear is that when disciples go out in dedicated mission, there may be consistent opposition and even hatred, but there are also new believers.

The second main aspect of the prayer is Jesus's request for his disciples' protection. Whereas most of our praying is along the perfectly legitimate lines of "give us today our bread for tomorrow", expressed in prayers for health, housing, jobs, family and exams, the focus of Jesus's prayer here is much more along the lines of "your kingdom come".

His prayer is that the disciples will form a community of witness to him in the world. As Jesus returns to the Father and will not be in the world for much longer, they will then become the living presence of Christ. Thus, he prays, "I will remain in the world no longer, but they are still in the world, and I am coming to you. Holy Father, protect them by the power of your name—the name you gave me—so that they may be one as we are one" (17:11). This protection is not physical, for we know that several of the disciples are martyred, but is protection from the "evil one" (17:15). In other words, it is a prayer that they might maintain their faith and unity in order to bear a valid and compelling witness to Christ as Lord and Saviour. When this prayer is lived out in the rubbish dumps of Cairo, the favelas of Brazil, the strife-filled communities of the Congo, or the slums in Kibera in Nairobi, it is a compelling witness bringing hope and love to often otherwise bleak and hope-less communities. Likewise, Christians in the materialist west need to be protected from the beckoning seduction of wealth, whether in the hills of Surrey, the squares of Belgravia, or the commercial heart of the City. Effective witness will come, wherever we are, by protection from all that compromises our witness and sanctification in the truth. This is in part the object of Jesus's prayer.

The future Church (17:20-26)

The final section of Jesus's prayer is directed at the future Church, that is, towards those who will believe in the testimony of the Apostles and subsequent believers. Once again, it is through hearing and understanding the message, literally the "word" (Greek: *logos*, meaning "word", see John 1:1), that new believers come into existence (17:20). Jesus's prayer for these subsequent believers is that they might be *one*, and more than that, that they may have the same unity the Father has with the Son. Evidence that these believers reside in the Father and Son will be a means of convincing the world (17:21). However, the disunity of the Church frustrates Jesus's prayer and jeopardizes the witness of the Church in every generation. Our only response to that must be repentance for the past and a commitment to unity in the present. Indeed, the inner character of God, which is his glory as well, and which combines perfect love with justice, is also the gift of God to the Church (17:22).

Rather than move on in his prayer, Jesus persists with his request that the Church in all its facets be brought to "complete unity" (17:23). (The word translated as "complete unity" is an interesting one—*tetelieōménoi*—meaning "fully mature in unity".) Once again, the effect of this unity is missionary: it enables the world to know in truth that the Father sent the Son and loves the Church (17:23). Presumably the reverse is also true: failure to display such mature unity means the world finds it harder to believe that the Son is sent by the Father, and evidence of the love of God for the Church is marred as well.

The universal and eternal nature of the prayer is further endorsed by Jesus's desire, expressed intimately to the Father, that his followers (those whom the Father gave him) see the full extent of his glory in the future, presumably in the resurrection, but also in the heavenly vision that awaits (see Revelation 4 and 5). Once again, the theme of glory, which is so present in the Gospel from the outset, is now fully extended (see 1:14 and 12:23ff.). The disciples are to see the full extent of the Son's glory, which he had with the Father before the foundation of the world. It is a glory which comes from the Father to the Son eternally, and which is given out of love for the Son by the Father (17:24). In other words, it is the final revelation of reality: the reality that underpins the existence of the universe. It is this reality that Jesus wants his followers to see, incontrovertibly and eternally.

The prayer is now about to end and in almost the same way in which it began (see 17:3), with the purpose of *knowing God* and *knowing or recognizing* his Son as being the mission of Jesus and the Father. The verb "to know" (Greek: *gnōridzō*) is used five times in two sentences, explaining the purpose of Jesus's coming as being that of spreading the knowledge of himself, the Son, sent by the Father. Indeed, at the outset of the Gospel, John says that although Jesus came to his own, to fellow Jews, they did not recognize or receive him, "Yet to all who received him, to those who believed in his name, he gave the right to become children of God, children born not of natural descent, nor of human decision or a husband's will, but born of God" (1:12,13). Jesus now affirms that he will go on making his true identity known to the disciples and with that and in that, he will also make known the love with which the Father loves the Son. Thus, knowledge brings with it the experience of love: it is not dry, dusty knowledge or information, but the knowledge of love that reaches into the core of human personality. In conclusion, one could then say that the life, love and knowledge that exists eternally in the Triune God will be eternally in them, the disciples, also. This surely is the infinite scope of the prayer.

Having concluded this prayer and teaching, Jesus walks off the Temple Mount, crosses the Kidron Valley, enters the Garden of Gethsemane, and continues to pray and wait with his sleepy disciples—for whom he has been praying (Luke 22:39ff.)—until his arrest, various trials and then crucifixion.

CHAPTER 19

Arrest, Trials, and Peter's Denial

John 18:1–19:16

Jesus now goes to Gethsemane, a garden on the Mount of Olives, to which he often retreats (18:2). It is a place of peace close to the crush and intensity of the city. While the Synoptic authors tell us of Jesus's struggle to accept the will of the Father as a cup of suffering that he must drink to the dregs (see Matthew 26:36–56; Mark 14:32–52; and Luke 22:39–53), John, having given us Jesus's great prayer in the Temple precincts, concentrates on his rather tawdry arrest.

Judas, who has already been identified by Jesus as his betrayer (see 13:26,27), now leads a posse of temple guards to this familiar place. The detachment of Jewish soldiers, together with some officials representing both the Chief Priests and the Pharisees, come with their torches, lanterns and weapons (18:3). At this point in John's account, it seems that Jesus takes the initiative. Whereas the Synoptic Gospels record the identification of Jesus by a combination of a greeting and a kiss from Judas (see Mark 14:44–45), in John's account it is Jesus who reveals himself to the posse.

The underlying motif of John's record of the arrest is the authority of Jesus in contrast to the moral weakness of the others. Jesus's authority is shown in a number of ways. Firstly, it is he who asks who they are looking for and then reveals his identity. He knows all that is to happen to him (18:4) so he does not hide from what is about to occur. Secondly, when he reveals himself as Jesus of Nazareth the men who have come to arrest him fall back to the ground. This is a further sign of the actual physical power of both his presence and his name. (I well remember confronting a man in our churchyard in Bath who was fighting with another, armed with a machete. I shouted, more instinctively than with any deliberation, "In the name of God, stop!" He at once dropped the machete and ran off! As the song goes, "there is power in the name of Jesus".)

And in the Garden of Gethsemane after the group have hauled themselves back to their feet, Jesus asks for a second time, "Who is it you want?" He replies to their request for Jesus of Nazareth (18:5a) with resonances of divinity, "I am he" (see also 8:58). Lastly, Jesus demands that if they are looking for him, they should let his disciples go, which they do. After all, although they will scatter, Jesus wants the disciples' lives preserved as they are to be the vanguard of the Church and the Kingdom of God on earth (18:8–9).

If on the one hand Jesus shows typical authority and presence of mind, on the other, the men in the story, whether friends or foes, reveal their shabbiness and self-interest. Having planted his kiss on Jesus to identify him—unnecessarily, as it happens, since Jesus has revealed himself—Judas stands guiltily by. The detachment of men recognize that they can do what they want under cover of darkness, since they lack the courage and the authority to do it openly (see 9:4b; 12:35; 13:30). And Peter, in a vain and peremptory attempt to prevent the stream of divinely planned history (18:11b), strikes out with his sword, slicing off the right ear of Malchus, the High Priest's servant. Jesus immediately heals the ear and tells Peter to put away his sword (18:11a). It is possible that Malchus is so named because he later becomes a disciple and a member of the Jerusalem church. Nonetheless, the instinctive bravado of Peter dissolves within hours when he finds himself denying any knowledge of Jesus. What is true of the arrest is thus also true of the whole passion narrative, i.e., the stark contrast between the nobility of Jesus, *the* Man and the self-interest of particular men, while the women prove consistently loyal.

The trials before the High Priests (18:12–14,19–24)

Although John divides the two trials or hearings of Jesus before Annas and Caiaphas with the denials of Simon Peter, we shall take these two events in the passion narrative of John separately. Jesus is first taken by the detachment of temple guards from Gethsemane back into the city and to the house of Annas in the Essene Quarter of Jerusalem near Herod's fortress. Annas is the father-in-law of Caiaphas, appointed High Priest in the newly formed Province of Judea by Quirinius, the Governor of Syria, from AD 6–15 (see Luke 2:2), who is based at Antioch, the principal Roman city of the region. Annas seems to be the main focus of Jewish power in Jerusalem, and we see him chairing the Sanhedrin when Peter and John are arraigned for healing the man at the Gate Beautiful (Acts 4:6). His son-in-law, Caiaphas, seems to be an instrument of the power of Annas, but is himself High Priest for a considerable length of time, possibly 15 years. What is clear is that a family controls the office of High Priest (Acts 4:6) and Jesus challenges this grip on power and the notion that Annas, who has five sons who will become High Priests, is a kind of High Priest Emeritus.

In any event, it is before Annas that the "trial" proceeds (18:19), until Jesus is taken, still bound, to Caiaphas (18:24), the actual High Priest, who has earlier prophesied that it is expedient for "one man to die for the people" (11:50; 18:14). The conduct of a Jewish trial such as this revolves around witness statements. Indeed, the idea of witness statements has been germane throughout the Gospel in establishing the identity of Jesus (see 5:31–40). Here the high priest Annas proceeds along the same lines. He seeks to indict Jesus based upon what others say about him, and, if possible, incriminate him on the basis of false teaching. Jesus will not be drawn about his teaching, saying that it was in the open, not in secret, spoken either in the synagogues or in the Temple. It was heard by all, and they could surely give an account of it (18:21). "Why question me? Ask those who heard me. Surely, they know what I said?" (18:21). Indeed, Jesus is calling upon Annas to find his own witnesses. Such a tone is considered impertinent, so one of the officials, no doubt with the intention of intimidation, strikes Jesus on the face. But Jesus will not back down, instead asking the court to testify what he has said wrong or whether he has spoken the truth. Once again in this Gospel, Jesus is concerned with the truth. Indeed, it is a continual refrain (see 8:32,44–45; 17:17) in the Gospel. Having come no closer to the truth, Jesus is taken from Annas's house to a full court hearing in the house of Caiaphas, the actual High Priest, where the entire Sanhedrin is present. Although not recorded by John, a full account of this trial, which appears to happen illegally overnight, may be found in both Matthew and Mark (Matthew 26:57ff., Mark 14:53ff. and Luke 22:66ff.). It is at this trial that false witnesses are brought against him, saying Jesus uses divine language about himself, provoking the charge of blasphemy. Meanwhile, outside both houses another drama is taking place from which Peter learns deep and searing lessons for his discipleship and leadership.

Peter's denial (18:15–18,25–26)

John presents Peter's denial in two parts. The denial could all have happened outside Annas's house, or could arguably have taken place between both high priests' houses. The Synoptic Gospel writers seem to make it clear that it took place outside the house of Caiaphas, as if that were the lengthier and more formal of the two High Priestly trials (Matthew 26:69ff., Mark 14:66ff. and Luke 22:54). Whatever the actual setting, we know that the denials take place in the High Priest's courtyard, where Peter now finds himself, having followed Jesus after his arrest. It seems that the other disciple with Peter (see 18:15) might well be John himself, who is somehow known to the High Priest's household and the High Priest Annas and his family as well. If so, John himself vouches for Peter and asks the girl on the gate to allow Peter into the courtyard of the house where Jesus is being detained and tried (18:16).

It is the girl on the gate who is the first to ask if Peter knows Jesus and whether he is one of the disciples. Caught off guard, unprepared for the events now in train, or just plain frightened, he briefly and perhaps thoughtlessly replies, "I am not" (18:17b). Perhaps even this answer is a conscious allusion to the divine name, "I am", and hence reveals the fragility of our humanity. His first denial made, Peter warms himself by the fire or brazier in the courtyard designed to keep the bystanders warm on a chilly night. As he is doing so, he is challenged again, and once again denies being a disciple of Jesus (18:25). Lastly, a relative of Malchus, whose ear Peter sliced off earlier in Gethsemane, and who was also in the garden, recognizes him and challenges him as one of Jesus's disciples. For the third time, Peter denies knowing and following Jesus, and at that moment the cock crows. John does not record, unlike the other Gospel writers, that Peter goes out of the courtyard and weeps bitterly, or that Jesus turns and looks straight at Peter after his third denial as in Luke (Matthew 26:75b, Mark 14:72 and Luke 22:61,62). John simply leaves the story with the third painful denial, although he will return to the trauma right at the end in the final conversation of the Gospel.

The fact that the denial by Peter is in each of the Gospels is simply a reminder to us all that we have feet of clay. However well-known or close to Jesus we may be, we are fragile, vulnerable and weak. We are capable of falling. Peter has just spent three years in utter proximity to Jesus, has sworn undying loyalty (13:37), eschewed prayerful preparation (Mark 14:37,38), is capable of emotional assertions (Luke 22:31–34), but is as spiritually fragile as a kitten. The story of Peter is there because it is a warning, but it is also there, as we shall see, as a drama of hope.

Weary from his overnight trial and painfully aware of Peter's denial and the fulfilment of his prediction, Jesus is taken to yet another hearing. This time it is before the Roman Governor, Pontius Pilate. It provokes one of the longest conversations in the Gospel.

The trial before Pilate (18:28–19:16)

Of all the Gospel accounts of the trials, John gives most emphasis and space to the trial of Jesus before Pilate and the ensuing conversation. It is, in fact, the last long conversation in the Gospel.

The trial before Pilate, if we can call it that, divides into two parts. The first concerns the veracity of the charges against Jesus; the second, unusually, is Pilate's attempt to release Jesus, having found no basis for a charge against him, but lacking the strength of character to do so.

After the overnight trials at Annas and Caiaphas's houses, Jesus is brought to the nearby Governor's Palace. Fastidious about ceremonial cleanliness, but uncaring about manipulating the Law to gain their ends, the leaders of the Jews will not enter the precincts of the palace, a Gentile house, for fear of making themselves ritually unclean (18:28). Pilate, as is the case in Roman justice, asks to know the charges against the prisoner, and on which of these Jesus is to be tried. The Jews refuse to state what the charges are, simply saying that he is a criminal! The reason, it transpires, for seeking Pilate's decision is that they are not allowed to execute a prisoner. They want the governor to try Jesus and find him guilty of sedition, for which there is a capital punishment (18:31). Pilate is thus left to conduct his own trial with no manifest charges agreed. He goes inside the palace and summons Jesus (18:33).

Knowing something of the case and the reputation of Jesus, Pilate asks with some justification, "Are you the King of the Jews?" (18:33). After all, it is the key question, although a Jew might have asked (and did) whether Jesus claimed to be the Messiah. For a Jew to claim to be the Messiah would be blasphemy. To claim to be a king would be sedition in Roman eyes, for the Romans and their subjects in the empire had no ultimate king but Caesar. As so often, Jesus will not be drawn, but asks a different question, "Is that your own idea?" (18:34). Pilate is riled at having been put in the position of trying a man against whom there are no charges (18:35), so changes tack and asks Jesus not *who* he is but *what he has done* to end up there.

Jesus now responds differently. He gives Pilate something to work with, saying, "my kingdom is not of this world." He accepts he has a kingdom, but it is a kingdom not based in this world. Nor does his kingdom have worldly standards by which its members fight violently to achieve their ends. Instead, they should put up their swords (18:36). Pilate is relieved to hear that Jesus claims to be a king. At least, it is a claim he is familiar with, along with its political implications. Jesus then extends his claim and the basis of his kingship by saying he has been born a king (see Matthew 2:2), and furthermore, that anyone on the side of truth will recognize his kingship. In fact, Jesus is saying that his authority is based in truth—one of the great themes of the Gospel—which precipitates another almost philosophical question from Pilate: "What is truth?" With that the trial is over, with Pilate concluding that there is no charge for Jesus to answer and saying he wants to release him (18:38–39). The rest of the "trial" is Pilate failing to do what he knows he should do, but is frightened to do, in itself a common human failing.

Pilate tries to release Jesus from the moment he decides that there is no charge to answer (18:38). Knowing that there is a custom where the governor releases a Jewish prisoner at Passover, he asks to release "the king of the Jews". But the Jewish leaders, who have by now whipped up the crowd, call instead for the release of Barabbas. (Barabbas is a Greek name derived from the Aramaic *Bar 'Abbā*, meaning, ironically, "Son of the Father".) Indeed, this whole sequence is full of irony, with Jesus mocked as though he were a king, when he really is one. Unable to release Jesus, Pilate has him flogged in the hope that this will prove sufficient punishment for the Jewish authorities. There are various levels of flogging, and it is thought by some this was the least severe, called the *fustigation*, the worst being called the *verberatio*, in which the flesh of the victim would hang like shreds from his back. However, Jesus is also mocked by the soldiers, who have "fun" with their victim. He is dressed in a purple robe denoting royalty, given a woven crown of thorns, and the false acclamation, "Hail, King of the Jews." He is then brought out onto the balcony to the assembled crowd, with Pilate shouting, "Here is the Man" (*Ecce Homo*, or in Greek, *idoù ò ánthrōpos*). This title, although uttered in irony, is full of truth. Here indeed is the paradigmatic man, the model for all humanity.

When the chief priests and their officials, the leaders of the Jewish hierarchy, hear this, they refuse to take Jesus back (19:6), only increasing their demand that he be crucified, the most frequent capital punishment used by the Romans. Initially Pilate refuses, saying, "you take him and crucify him. As for me, I find no basis for a charge against him" (19:6b), but the leaders reply that Jesus has claimed to be the Son of God, and that claim, blasphemous if not true, is punishable by death. Far from reassuring Pilate that there are reasonable grounds for punishment, this only makes him more "afraid" (19:8). He once more goes inside, and with this claim of divinity ringing in his ears, understandably asks Jesus where he comes from. But Jesus will not be drawn into answering that question (19:9). Pressed to answer, with Pilate saying he has the power to release him, Jesus unnervingly answers that Pilate would have no power had it not been vested in him, not by the Emperor Tiberius, but "from above", i.e., from God himself.

From this point onwards it is simply a contest of wills. Pilate wants to release Jesus even more (19:12). The Jewish leaders, on the other hand, become increasingly insistent that Jesus be crucified. Their argument is devastatingly simple and politically powerful: "If you let this man go you are no friend of Caesar." The punchline, "Anyone who claims to be a king opposes Caesar" (19:12b), is the clincher. The remaining part of the narrative is all about Pilate dressing up what he knows to be wrong both morally and legally, which is his reluctant acquiescence to the High Priests' desires.

Pilate once more comes outside. In another Gospel, Pilate washes his hands at this point, trying to absolve himself of responsibility for the death of Jesus (Matthew 27:24). Furthermore, Pilate also receives a message from his wife, who declares Jesus innocent and tells her husband that she has "suffered a great deal today in a dream because of him" (Matthew 27:19). Nevertheless, however reluctantly, Pilate takes a seat on the place called Gabbatha, which is a stone pavement that can still be viewed today. It is nearly the sixth hour or midday. In part to infuriate the Jews, Pilate calls out, "Here is your King." Never was a truer word spoken in jest. They respond, "Take him away, crucify him" (19:15). And to Pilate's riposte, "Shall I crucify your king?", they reply with underlying sarcasm, "We have no king but Caesar" (19:15). At this, Pilate hands Jesus over to the soldiers to be crucified. The die is cast.

All of the trials exhibit the tawdriness of human sinfulness: the envy and deceit of the High Priests and their officials; the salacious cruelty of Herod, which is not recorded in John's Gospel (see Luke 23:6ff.); and then the cowardice of Pilate, who refuses to face down the crowd and the false motives of the High Priests, although Pilate recognizes more than many the truth that is in Jesus. Before them all Jesus remains the model of restraint and dignity. He is now ready for his glory to be manifested as he is taken away to be crucified.

CHAPTER 20

The Crucifixion

John 19:16b–42

Each of the Gospel presentations of the crucifixion differ in some of the details. Furthermore, each presentation in some respects echoes the chief themes of that particular Gospel. Matthew and Mark choose to recall the final taunts between the Jewish establishment and Jesus, even as he dies on the cross. The Chief Priests and the teachers of the Law thus mock Jesus as he dies pinned to the cross, saying, "He saved others, but he can't save himself! He's the King of Israel! Let him come down now from the cross, and we will believe in him" (Matthew 27:41ff.; Mark 15:31,32). Once again, Matthew highlights the way Jesus fulfils Old Testament Scripture by recording the great cry of dereliction, "My God, my God, why have you forsaken me?" (Matthew 27:46), which is uttered by Jesus during the darkest period of his crucifixion. Matthew thus demonstrates both the fulfilment of the prophetic Psalm 22 in Jesus's crucifixion and the complete estrangement between the authorities and Jesus.

Mark similarly recalls the taunting by the Chief Priests and the teachers of the Law and the cry of dereliction. But, since he writes his Gospel quite probably in Rome and in light of Peter's reminiscences, he also tells of the Roman centurion's reaction to Jesus's death, namely: "Surely this man was the Son of God" (Mark 15:39).

Luke recalls many of the same details: the mocking, the written notice above the cross saying, "This is the King of the Jews", and the action of the soldiers. Luke also typically chooses to record the conversation between the dying criminals and Jesus: one defiant, the other penitent. Luke writes a Gospel that persistently includes the outsider, the estranged and the overlooked, and demonstrates the grace that Jesus has come to offer such people. He makes this clear even in his account of the crucifixion.

John's account of the crucifixion is both sparing and profound. All the Evangelists have two parts to their accounts. The first section generally involves the walk with the cross to Golgotha, with Jesus being helped by Simon of Cyrene (Matthew and Mark); the actual crucifixion, with the affixing of a notice to the upright calling Jesus King of the Jews; the mockery of the Jewish leaders; and the gambling by the soldiers for Jesus's clothes. The second part of the narrative begins with growing darkness, then the most agonized words from the cross, the sense of Jesus's abandonment even by his Father, and the differing responses of the bystanders. If we are to isolate any themes from John's telling of the crucifixion, then we notice both the humanity and majesty of Jesus, his life-giving words and death.

Manhood and majesty (19:16b-27)

The walk from the Royal Palace or Praetorium in Jerusalem to Golgotha, just outside the old walls of the city, re-built by Herod the Great like so much else, is not very far. It is about a kilometre, but for a prisoner who has been flogged and up all night at various trials, every step would be excruciating. Other Gospel writers tell us that a passer-by, one Simon of Cyrene, is forced to carry Jesus's cross to the place of execution. There, at the place of the skull, Jesus is crucified along with two others. Nails are hammered through his hands and feet into the cross beam and the upright, and then the cross, with the victim on it, is hoisted into a hole with an awful jolt, jarring the newly made wounds. From then on, every breath is a struggle. Affixed to the cross and above Jesus's head is a notice written in three languages—Aramaic, Greek and Latin—so that the entire ancient world might know. It reads: "Jesus of Nazareth, the King of the Jews." The Chief Priests and the Jews object to this ascription. It is too definite, too much like a proclamation, but indubitably it is the idea of Pilate, who has recognized the majesty of Jesus, but does not have the courage to acquit him publicly of the sketchy charges which he knows in his heart are bogus. On this point, Pilate remains unmoved, declaring:

"What I have written, I have written" (19:22). It is as if this Gentile is proclaiming the majesty of Jesus, saying that his throne is to be the cross, from where he will form a new community.

As Jesus hangs on the cross naked, the soldiers gamble for his clothes. It seems there are four soldiers in the execution squad or quaternion. They are inured to crucifixion, the most common and brutal form of Roman punishment. Also, the number four in John's writings, and especially in Revelation, represents the universal community, i.e., every nation, tribe, people and language (Revelation 7:9). The clothing of Jesus thus represents his all-sufficient sacrifice. Furthermore, the seamless robe, representing the High Priest's garment, underlines the seamless sacrifice made by this High Priest which is both eternal and universal (see Hebrews 7:27ff. and 9:12–14).

Lastly, in this first part of the crucifixion before darkness falls and the desolate agony of an abandoned Son becomes apparent, in one of his earlier utterances from the cross—like his forgiveness of the soldiers and his conversation with the two thieves (see Luke 23:34 and Luke 23:39ff.)—Jesus speaks to his mother and Beloved Disciple. It seems John, the Beloved Disciple, unlike the rest, stays close to Jesus with Mary, the Mother of Jesus. In fact, the three Marys stand close by the cross: Mary the Mother of Jesus, Mary Clopas, her sister, and Mary Magdalene (19:25). Addressing his mother first, he says, "woman" (19:26, Greek: *gúnai*, "woman" as in 2:4) "here is your son", and to John he says, "Here is your mother" (19:27). Not only is it extraordinary that in such a moment of extremis Jesus takes thought and care of his mother, but also from that moment John takes care of Mary (19:27b). It is not an exaggeration to say that a new family or community is formed at the cross.

The depths of the cross (19:28–37)

We come now to the second sequence of events at the cross and two sayings or words spoken in swift succession. There are seven sayings from the cross: to the soldiers, "Father forgive them for they do not know what they are doing" (Luke 23:34); to the penitent thief, "I tell you the truth, today you will be with me in paradise" (Luke 23:43); to Mary and to John,

"Woman, here is your son" and "Here is your mother" (19:26b,27); to the Father, "My God, My God why have you forsaken me?" (Matthew 27:46 and Mark 15:34); to the bystanders, "I am thirsty" (19:28); to the world, "It is finished" (19:30); and finally to his Father again, "Father, into your hands I commit my Spirit" (Luke 23:46). In these words, in the Gospel, John demonstrates the suffering of the incarnate Lord.

Firstly, only John records the cry of Jesus, "I am thirsty" (19:28). As Gregory Nazianzus recalls in his *Oration on the Son* in Constantinople in AD 379: Jesus, the one who previously offers water to all those who are thirsty, now himself as man thirsts. Jesus is offered cheap wine (vinegar) on a sponge-like plant ready for those who are suffering. On this occasion, having been offered wine mixed with myrrh previously (Matthew 27:34; Mark 15:23; Luke 23:36), Jesus drinks. Soon after receiving the final drink, Jesus utters his penultimate cry, "It is finished." By all accounts, it is a loud cry, of completion, even of triumph, having drunk the cup of suffering for human sin to its dregs. The Greek word *tetélestai*, translated as "it is finished", is often used as an indication that a debt has been paid. At this moment, Jesus bows his head—surely an eyewitness detail—and delivers up his Spirit (19:30). John gives us the impression throughout that Jesus remains in charge, even choosing his moment of death (see 10:18).

At this point, there is a sequence of events which confirms the death of Jesus. Once again, the fastidious legalism of the Jewish hierarchy comes to the fore. Just as they will not break their rules of ceremonial purity by entering the governor's palace (18:28), but are content to manipulate laws of evidence to charge and condemn Jesus, having achieved the death of Jesus they now do not want his body remaining on a cross and so disfiguring the Feast of Passover. Consequently, they ask Pilate to hasten the deaths of the victims by breaking their legs, so that they can no longer heave themselves up on their crosses to take a breath, and so in effect suffocate. Having first broken the legs of the two thieves or criminals, and hence hastening their death and ending their misery, the soldiers come to Jesus. Seeing from his posture that he is already dead and that there are no signs of life, one of the soldiers thrusts a spear into his side. Fluid that looks like blood and water comes out. This is either evidence of a ruptured heart leading to a separation of blood clot and serum, or it might be a more symbolic point, so beloved of John, that from Jesus's sacrifice comes forth both life-giving water (see 7:37–39) and cleansing sacrificial blood. Indeed, it may well have both meanings in the mind of the Evangelist, in that way underlining the reality of Jesus's death, but also its life-giving, redemptive nature.

Lastly, like all the Evangelists in different ways, John affirms that the death of Jesus fulfils Old Testament Scripture. First, like the Passover Lamb in Exodus, none of Jesus's bones are broken (see Exodus 12:46), since, as with the righteous man in Psalm 34, all of his bones are protected by God (see Psalm 34:20). Secondly, John adds that Jesus's crucifixion will fulfil the prophet Zechariah's words that "they will look on me, the one they have pierced, and they will mourn . . . bitterly" (Zechariah 12:10). Thus, like Matthew, Mark and Luke, John, who is writing about 60 years after the events, reflects that the crucifixion is God's long-prepared answer to human guilt and is signalled frequently as such in the Hebrew Scriptures. Jesus himself makes this plain (see Luke 24:45–47). Having shown us unequivocally that Jesus dies and has finished paying for human guilt, John completes his narrative with a very personal description of Jesus's burial.

The burial of Jesus's body (19:38–42)

The burial of Jesus's body is the essential sequel to the crucifixion and also the prequel to the resurrection. From the very start, John has made it clear in the Prologue that the Word becomes flesh, that the Son of God takes on human form (1:14). Far from despising or denigrating the body or the flesh, as some Greek philosophy does, and as Gnostic teaching is soon to do just a few years after John's writing, the Gospel of John shows that God inhabits a human body; he becomes flesh. Although Jesus commends his spirit into the hands of his Father at the point of death (see 19:30 and Luke 23:46), his resurrection will be bodily. In other words, his human body will be swallowed up in a resurrection body in continuity with his earthly human body, but also entirely new (see Paul's explanation of this in 1 Corinthians 15:50–58).

Thus, with the spirit of Jesus safely with the Father from the point of his death, the earthly body of Jesus must be cared for in preparation for resurrection. Step forward Joseph of Arimathea and Nicodemus. Joseph of Arimathea is a rich and influential man, probably from Judea, although Arimathea has not been precisely located. A member of the Sanhedrin like Nicodemus, and a disciple of Jesus, although hitherto in secret, he now boldly approaches Pilate for the body of Jesus, to care for it and bury it with dignity (19:38,39). Joseph is to supply the tomb, his own, and Nicodemus provides an ample supply of 75 pounds of spices and burial linen. The body of Jesus is released by Pilate and given to Joseph, whereupon the two wrap it with strips of linen and spices (19:40). This, we are told, indicates the dignity and respect shown to the body of the deceased customary in Jewish, and later Christian, obsequies or funeral rites.

Curiously, as I write this on Sunday, 11 September 2022, the body of Her Late Majesty Queen Elizabeth II (1926–2022) is being moved from Balmoral Castle to Edinburgh and then later to London. Thousands are lining the route to pay their respects. The body is the last physical point of contact with a person being mourned. Although lifeless, it gives an opportunity and necessary focus for grief or mourning, and so helps in coming to terms with the loss of another who is loved and respected. Jesus's body is taken by some of those who love him, like several of his women followers (Luke 23:55,56; Mark 15:47; Matthew 27:61), and in their presence is entombed in a new tomb hewn out of rock belonging to Joseph of Arimathea. The garden in which Jesus is buried is close by Golgotha and because sundown and the beginning of the Sabbath are approaching, they bury him quickly but decently, with love and care. Jesus has all but completed his mission on earth. His body lies in the grave. His spirit rests with the Father but in some way still active (see 1 Peter 3:18–20). Humanity and creation wait for the early hours of Sunday morning when the body of Jesus will disappear and a new triumphant, resurrected Christ will show himself to his followers and to the world. A new beginning for the created order and the history of the universe is about to take place.

CHAPTER 21

The Day of Resurrection

John 20:1–31

Each Evangelist has their own way of telling the story of the resurrection. As always, the Gospels tell us the details of the event, the story with its human consequences. It is left to the Epistles to draw out the theological significance for humanity and the whole of creation. Passages like Romans 8:18–39 and 1 Corinthians 15 do this.

Matthew has a brief account (Matthew 28:1–20), mostly centred on the empty tomb and the message of the angel. Mark has a truncated end to his Gospel (Mark 16:1–8), as if it has been lost or cut short by an interruption. Luke and John have the longest and most varied accounts, with Luke giving the most space to the wonderful walk to Emmaus and the revelation of Jesus in the breaking of bread (Luke 24:13–35). At the heart of John's narrative are conversations between Jesus and Mary Magdalene and between Jesus and Simon Peter. In fact, John 20 is essentially about the reality of the resurrection, whereas the concluding chapter of John 21 is the Epilogue, balancing the Prologue, and is about the mission of the Church.

At first light (20:1–9)

The central witness of this chapter is Mary Magdalene. She is the first to discover the empty tomb and the first to encounter the risen Jesus. At the earliest opportunity after the Sabbath, while it is dark, she makes her way to the tomb with other women. She has seen the body buried there on Friday evening and no doubt that scene and the preceding crucifixion are etched on her heart and memory (Matthew 27:61). Her mind and emotions are fixed on those events throughout the next two nights. Barely able to sleep, as soon as she can do so safely without breaking the Jewish Sabbath, she goes to the garden where Jesus has been laid to rest. In the clearing darkness and at first light, she sees that the stone over the mouth of the tomb has been rolled away. Without pausing to glean anything more, she runs to where she knows Simon Peter is and tells him this unexpected news: "They have taken the Lord out of the tomb, and we [presumably the other women with her, see Luke 24:1] don't know where they have put him!" (20:2).

Peter and the Beloved Disciple immediately run to the tomb themselves. John, perhaps the younger and fitter man, outruns Peter and reaches the tomb first. He sees the linen strips lying there but does not go in (20:4,5), while Peter typically pushes past and enters the tomb, where he sees the same sight. The burial cloths seem to suggest a message: probably rolled like a chrysalis around the body with spices interleaved between their folds, they are now seemingly deflated, as if the body has risen through them, leaving them entwined but empty. And to one side is the burial cloth that surrounded Jesus's head (20:6,7). Such is the manner in which the cloths lie, plus the reality of the empty tomb and possibly the recollection of Jesus's own words that he will rise again, that these things converge in John's mind to trigger a spark of belief or an epiphany of faith. In a telling Johannine phrase, we are told that "he saw and believed" (20:8b). This is the essential and necessary reaction to the resurrection of the Word made flesh (see 1:12, 6:29). It is the human response that the incarnation, crucifixion and resurrection expect and demand, that we believe. As yet, John's faith and especially Peter's is only half-formed, for they do not fully understand "that Jesus had to rise from the dead" (20:9). Meanwhile, Mary Magdalene weeps outside the tomb while the other disciples go "back to their homes" (20:10).

The first witness, Mary Magdalene (20:10–18)

As I write this, the country is in deep national mourning for the late Queen Elizabeth II. As the late Queen herself said after the 9/11 attacks, grief is the other side of love. Mary, like John, has looked inside the tomb, but perhaps only cursorily, and is still under the impression, as she later says to "the gardener", that Jesus's body has been stolen, although curiously anything of any value has been left in the tomb. At the same time, as she looks again, she sees two angels. What they look like is conjecture, but possibly not like the angel described by Matthew as having an appearance "like lightning, and his clothes were white as snow" (Matthew 28:3), otherwise the angels would have made a greater impression on her and forestalled her question of them. Perhaps the angels looked more like Mark's description of "a young man dressed in a white robe" (Mark 16:5), or again like Luke's description of "two men in clothes that gleamed like lightning stood beside them" (the women) (Luke 24:4). Whatever their appearance, and however arresting, Mary is literally so blinded by her grief that she persists with her original assumption that the body has been taken. She responds to the angels who ask why she is weeping that, "they have taken my Lord away and I don't know where they have put him" (20:13b). As C. S. Lewis wrote in *A Grief Observed*, a grief can blot every other feeling:

> Where is God? This is one of the most disquieting symptoms. When you are happy, so happy that you have no sense of needing him, so happy that you are tempted to feel his claims upon you as an interruption, if you remember yourself and turn to him with gratitude and praise, you will be—or so it feels—welcomed with open arms. But go to him when your need is desperate, with all other help in vain, and what do you find? A door slammed in your face, and a sound of bolting and double bolting on the inside. After that, silence. You may as well turn away. The longer you wait, the more emphatic the silence will become. There are no lights in the windows. Why is he so present a commander in our time of prosperity and so very absent a help in time of trouble?[68]

Mary's grief overcomes the message of the grave clothes, overlays the enquiry of the two men dressed to be noticed in the tomb at the head and foot of where the body lay, and finally masks even the presence of Jesus until he addresses her by name.

---

[68]   C. S. Lewis, *A Grief Observed* (London: Faber, 1973), p. 9.

At this point in the narrative, one of the great ironies of the resurrection appearances takes place, equalled only by the two disciples walking with "a stranger" to Emmaus and telling him the story of the last few days in Jerusalem (Luke 24:13ff.), when this stranger is himself the story. On this occasion, turning away from the tomb and still weeping, Mary catches sight of a man she thinks is the gardener. He too asks why she is crying and who she is looking for (or literally, "who do you seek?", 20:15). But Mary, believing him to be the gardener responsible for taking the body of Jesus, asks him where he has put it.

It is when Jesus utters Mary's name that recognition comes. A single use of her name in a style typical of Jesus's speech provokes instant recognition. It is said that our voices are as distinctive as our handwriting or our fingerprints, so much so that banks now confidently identify their customers simply by their voices. In an instant, Mary realizes that the gardener is in fact Jesus, alive and risen from the dead. She cries out in exultant joy, "Rabboni" (meaning "teacher"), and holds him close. But something has changed. It is not so much a time for holding as a time for going. Jesus has not yet ascended to his Father, so he will be seen by his followers again, but soon he will return to his Father. In the meantime, Mary has a job to do, a command to follow, which is that she should tell Jesus's brothers (interesting that the disciples are for the first time called brothers) that he is "returning to my Father and your Father, to my God and your God" (20:17). In other words, the message is that Jesus has completed his task. The Word made flesh who was in the beginning with God and was God is now returning home (1:1–2). The mission is complete. Redemption is finished (19:30). The Father has been made known by the Son (14:9) and now the Spirit will make these things real in the hearts of the disciples (14:26). As instructed, Mary returns to the disciples and says, "I have seen the Lord" (20:18). It will not be long before Jesus appears to almost all the disciples or Apostles together.

The evening of the first day and preparing for the future (20:19–23)

The disciples do not have long to wait. Fearful of the Jewish authorities, they are assembled behind locked doors when Jesus suddenly appears among them. His body is similar and different, and he needs to reassure the disciples that it really is him. He greets them by saying, "peace be with you!" (Greek for "peace": *ei'rēnē*, from which we get "irenic"). Having said this to reassure them, he further calms them by showing them his hands and side: his hands wounded by the nails and his side injured by the spear thrust, which they were sure to have heard about. Rightly, the disciples are overjoyed at his appearance, although not yet fully understanding.

Jesus reiterates his greeting of peace and then immediately prepares the disciples for the mission ahead. Using a formula that has become so well known in John's Gospel, in which the Father's relationship with Jesus is a pattern for Jesus's relationship with us, he outlines the mission ahead. Just as Jesus was sent by the Father to reveal him, his love and purpose to the world, so now the disciples are likewise to be sent by Jesus into the world to reveal the Father and the Son. Furthermore, he equips them for the task and authorizes them to forgive sins.

In a symbolic action, Jesus breathes over the disciples and says, "Receive the Holy Spirit." The Spirit has already been described as being like breath or wind in the Gospel (see 3:8) and is likewise perceived as the breath of God in the creation in Genesis, in the revival of Israel in Ezekiel, and at Pentecost (see Genesis 2:7; Ezekiel 37:1–14; Acts 2:2a). Now Jesus breathes on them, indicating that they are to receive the Spirit, which they do in reality on the day of Pentecost (Acts 1:8; 2:4). This will equip them for the task of mission. Central to that mission was and is the proclamation of forgiveness. Thus, Jesus authorizes the disciples, and through them the Church, to pronounce in his name the forgiveness of sins.

There is no doubt that forgiveness is at the heart of the Gospel message. When the birth of Jesus is announced to Joseph, he is told that the child to be born is to be called Jesus "because he will *save his people from their sins*" (Matthew 1:21). And Luke tells us at the end of his Gospel that Jesus explains to the disciples that, "The Christ will suffer and rise from the dead on the third day, *and repentance and forgiveness of sins* will be preached in his name to all nations, beginning at Jerusalem" (Luke 24:46–47). Paul wonderfully tells us in his prayer at the beginning of his Epistle to the Colossians that, "He has rescued us from the dominion of darkness and brought us into the kingdom of the Son he loves in whom we have redemption, *the forgiveness of sins*" (Colossians 1:13,14). Forgiveness quite simply means *release* from the penalty and power of sin or the self-life, both its actions and its internal dominion of desires. For its part, the Church is to proclaim and declare this forgiveness to people in its preaching and example, as well as in personal terms wherever there is repentance (a willingness to change, if not the power to do so). Jesus bequeaths singular authority to the Church to pronounce or withhold forgiveness in Christ's name. The condition of forgiveness in the New Testament is clear: repentance and faith in Jesus the Messiah (Christ) (see Acts 2:38–39). To accomplish this mission in the world in every generation the Spirit is needed, hence Jesus symbolically breathes the Spirit upon the disciples and this prophetic action is fulfilled in real time at Pentecost.

Examples of forgiveness, and its power to inspire both the Church and society, are scattered through the annals of Church history and its mission. Just as those who give up everything to follow Christ inspire and challenge the Church and the world (e.g., a Mother Teresa or a St Francis), likewise a Gordon Wilson or Phan Thi Kim Phúc inspire the Church to follow the often-painful path of forgiveness. Gordon Wilson, an Irish senator, forgave the IRA terrorists responsible for the murder of his daughter Marie, a student nurse, at a Remembrance Day bombing at Enniskillen in 1987. For her part, Kim Phúc forgave the pilot responsible for leading the US Airforce sortie which destroyed her village in Vietnam with napalm in 1972, and covered her with burns as she fled naked down the road. Surely a willingness to forgive, and the proclamation of forgiveness, lie at the heart of Christian discipleship. Thus, the risen Jesus prepares his disciples for the task of proclaiming forgiveness in his name and gives them the power to do so in the Holy Spirit. But not every disciple is there. Thomas is missing.

A week later (20:24-29)

From the little we hear of Thomas in John's Gospel, he seems an interesting character. Like a blunt Yorkshireman, he seems to be willing to express his objections or scepticism with colourful language. He appears on three separate occasions in the Gospel. Firstly, it is he who says with some bravado that he is ready to die with Jesus (11:16) when Jesus proposes to return to Judea, where he has recently been threatened (see 10:31ff.). Secondly, alone among the disciples, it is he who says to Jesus that "we do not know where you are going, so how can we know the way?" (14:5). And it is now Thomas, in the face of the enthusiastic, indeed ecstatic, report and account of Jesus being alive and risen from the dead, who will not believe: "Unless I see the nail marks in his hands and put my finger where the nails were, and put my hand into his side, I will not believe it" (20:25). Here is doubt, but not so much the common doubt of being in two minds, or not being able to quite summon belief, as in the man who says, "I believe but help my unbelief" (Mark 9:24). This is doubt as defiance. After all, Thomas's objection to the overwhelming evidence of the disciples' witness is that they appeared to have a sort of collective hysteria. It is a defiance that Jesus is well able to deal with.

A week later the disciples are together, and despite the resurrection the doors are still locked. Jesus accepts the challenge and offers Thomas the opportunity of placing his finger in the wounds of the nails in his hands and of putting his hand into his side. Of course, there is no need to do so. Thomas is overwhelmed, humbled and changed. He can only say, "My Lord and my God" (20:28). Accepting his worship, Jesus makes a contrast which must have humbled Thomas further by saying in effect, it took sight for you to believe but "blessed are those who have not seen and yet have believed" (20:29). In fairness to Thomas, he later goes out as a missionary and puts all his innate stubbornness and determination to good use in founding the church in Kerala, South India.

Summary (20:29–31)

Thomas's confession is a fitting start to the concluding passage of the Gospel, which now looks forward to those who will believe in the future, and so will be blessed. Then John makes some summary conclusions before the Epilogue of Chapter 21, which functions as a balance the Prologue. He concludes this chapter and the main narrative of the Gospel by saying that Jesus performed "many other miraculous signs . . . which are not recorded in this book" (20:30). John comes here to the crux of the Gospel's intention, which is that all its readers might believe—the great verb of the Gospel—and in believing may receive "life" (Greek: *zoe*) in his name. Indeed, the purpose of the Word becoming flesh is not only to show God to the world, but to offer the opportunity of finding life in all its fullness (10:10).

CHAPTER 22

The Epilogue: The World Awaits

John 21:1–25

We know that the resurrection appearances occur over a 40-day period from the first Easter Day (Acts 1:3b) to the Ascension of Christ (see Acts 1:9 and Luke 24:51). Jesus's appearance on the shore of Lake Galilee must take place some days after the second appearance to the disciples, at which Thomas is present (20:24ff.). Despite the empty tomb and the appearances of Jesus to the disciples and Mary Magdalene, the mood of the narrative indicates a certain listlessness among the disciples while they wait in Galilee. Following the instruction of Jesus to the women (see Matthew 28:7), they have journeyed from Jerusalem to Galilee, surely a four- or five-day walk. Once back in Galilee, and with a chance to process the significance of the resurrection, they appear uncertain what to do next. It will take the words of Jesus and the power of the Spirit to initiate the world-wide mission which the Epilogue supposes. In the context of this listlessness, Peter the activist, unable to sit around anymore, says to the disciples, "I am going fishing", inviting the others to go with him (21:3).

They go out to fish on the Sea of Tiberias (21:1), the Romanized name for Lake Galilee, re-named after Tiberias, the emperor at that time. Tiberius succeeded Augustus in AD 14 and ruled in an ever more desultory way until AD 37, some years after the resurrection. If John is writing his Gospel in Ephesus around AD 90, this re-naming of Galilee as the Sea of Tiberias gives the narrative a more universal place in history. Perhaps that in itself is a nuanced way of saying that the life of Jesus is for the whole world (see Matthew 28:19,20 and Luke 24:47).

Some of his companions decide to go with Peter and a party of seven assemble to fish, including several who are well known in the Gospel, like Thomas, also called Didymus, meaning "twin"; Nathanael from Cana, who makes his first appearance in the Gospel at its start (see 1:45) and now at the finish; the sons of Zebedee, which include John the Beloved Disciple and James his brother and two other disciples, who may or may not have been part of the Twelve. They go out fishing and catch nothing (21:3b). The fruitlessness of the expedition matches their listlessness, until, that is, a stranger addresses them from the shore. The fruitlessness of their overnight fishing will be contrasted with their success in having listened to this "stranger".

A stranger on the shore (21:4–14)

Some make the case that fishermen in those days conventionally threw their nets on the left side of the boat, and that throwing them out on the right side would be unusual. Whether that is right or not, Jesus, having heard that they have caught "nothing", instructs them to throw the nets out on the right-hand side. Perhaps they are so despondent at the fruitlessness of the trip that they are willing to try anything before coming ashore. And this stranger, who they do not recognize as Jesus, appears to have some certainty or knowledge. They cast their nets on the right-hand side and immediately feel the tug of a very large catch. At this moment, there must be a sense of *déjà vu*, since at the time of their call, and particularly the call of Simon Peter, the disciples, having caught nothing all night, also make a very large catch under the instructions of Jesus (see Luke 5:1–11).

Once again it is because of his spiritual insight, as at the entrance of the tomb (see 20:8), that the Beloved Disciple recognizes Jesus. He shouts out in excitement, "It is the Lord!" (21:7). As soon as Simon Peter hears this, he replaces his outer garment, which he has taken off for fishing, and, since they are close to the shore, he jumps into the water. The remaining disciples make it to the shore in the boat, dragging the net full of fish behind them. They are just 90 metres from land. When they arrive, they see a fire already burning with fish being barbecued and bread nearby.

Jesus asks them to add some of the 153 fish they have just caught to the breakfast he is cooking. Not only has Jesus instructed them in their catch but now has prepared a breakfast for seven hungry men who have been out all night. Simon re-enters the boat and with the others drags the net with the 153 fish to the shore (21:11). Jesus takes the fish and bread, and in his usual manner gives thanks and distributes it to the disciples. Such is the occasion that it is eaten in silence. Awed by the presence of the risen Jesus and probably dumbfounded by the miraculous catch, they do not want to break the sense of mystery by saying something inappropriate.

For those reflecting on this event, there are several lessons for the mission of the Church in the world. Such mission, which in reality belongs to God, will only be effective and fruitful if directed by Christ, for "apart from me you can do nothing" (15:5b). If Jesus directs us, he also sustains us in that mission, demonstrating this by his care for the disciples in preparing food for them on the shore. Lastly, by working together, and using the resources given to us, we may effectively nurture the expanding community without breaking the nets of pastoral care. Now the Gospel ends, not on a note of triumphant expansion as it might have, but with a final conversation between Jesus and his leading disciple, Simon Peter. For Jesus, it seems, restoration is as important as expansion, fulfilling vocation as extending salvation. In other words, Jesus does not want to weave a rope of sand, but one which holds in the storm.

The reinstatement of Peter (21:15-21)

While it must be a conversation Peter is not looking forward to, it is still a necessity. When the silent breakfast is over, Jesus presumably beckons to Peter, and they walk and talk together (see 21:20). Going a little distance from the others, Jesus begins the interview directly and formally. Using Peter's full name, he speaks to the raw centre of Peter's identity, asking him, "Simon, son of John, do you love me more than these?" (21:15).

Initially in the conversation, indeed in the first two questions, the word Jesus uses for "love" is *agapaō*, i.e., self-giving love. But throughout the conversation Peter uses the different love word, *philéo*, meaning to love "as a friend". However, since the conversation is almost certainly originally conducted in Aramaic and not in Greek, we cannot build too much on this.

The question itself seems to have two parts: whether Peter loves Jesus, and second and more difficult, if he loves him *more than these*. Instinctively, Peter gives his replies, "Yes Lord, you know that I love you." Perhaps not trusting himself to answer directly, he implies that Jesus already knows the answer. At this, Jesus commissions him to feed his lambs, meaning the infant flock of God. Again, Jesus asks the question, "Simon, son of John, do you truly love me?" Peter replies with the same words and Jesus again charges him to look after his little sheep.

For a third time Jesus asks the question, but now uses the same word for love as Peter (i.e., *philéo*, 21:17). Now we understand that Jesus is meeting Peter's three denials with three opportunities to declare his love. He is cauterizing the wound effected by Peter's denials. Peter is nevertheless hurt by this third question. He answers it in the same way, but with more emphasis, "Lord you know all things; you know that I love you" (21:17). Once more Peter is commissioned to feed the flock of God, an epithet for the Church, and one that Peter himself will frequently use in his letters (see 1 Peter 2:25; 5:2ff.). And later, in that same Epistle, Peter will acknowledge that his sheep or followers love Jesus with the full self-giving loving of *agapaō* (see 1 Peter 1:8) despite never having seen him in the flesh.

As soon as Peter has answered for the third time, Jesus shows him the cost of his vocation and calling. There will come a time, says Jesus, predicting the future, when Peter will not be a free agent. He will go where he does not want to go, and be restrained and bound by others. It is commonly thought that this a reference to Peter's awaiting martyrdom. For the Early Church, the reference to Peter's hands being stretched out is a reference to crucifixion (21:18). Indeed, as editor, John purposefully says that this phrase refers to the type of death Peter will suffer. Finally, Jesus sums up all that he has said to Peter with the simple command, "Follow me". It is the short and the long of Christian discipleship and it echoes the words of his original calling (see Luke 5:11 and Mark 1:17). To be a Christian is to follow not an ideology, but a person. At that moment, Peter turns and catches sight of the Beloved Disciple, clearly identified as the one who leant back against Jesus at the Last Supper (13:23), and asks Jesus, "what about him?"

Final words (21:22–25)

The question "What about him or her?" is one that Jesus never answers. The reply comes back, "What is that to you?" In other words, Jesus's reply means "what concern is that of yours?" If the main thing is to "follow", we do not have to concern ourselves with what that means for others. Quite clearly Peter need not concern himself with what will happen to John. As it happens, John dies a very old man in Ephesus, having served as an exiled labourer on Patmos, where he receives a spectacular vision or revelation (see Revelation 1:9). Peter himself will most probably die in Rome as a martyr under Nero's persecution of the Church in c.AD 64. As Jesus makes clear to Peter, "If I want him to remain until I return [not knowing when that might be, see Matthew 24:36], what is that to you? You must follow me" (21:22). However, even then the rumour-mill of the Church (do things change?) is good at exaggerating or magnifying Jesus's words. What appears to get out, and is perhaps widely believed, even when John is writing this Gospel in c.AD 90, is that he will not die, but perhaps, like Elijah, be taken up to heaven (see 2 Kings 2:11–12). John takes the opportunity to clarify what Jesus has said (21:23b). Likewise, we are to be concerned with our own discipleship primarily, and our own course, rather than look over our shoulders at others.

Finally, John tells us indirectly that it is the Beloved Disciple who has written down this Gospel and account of Jesus's life (21:24). His testimony is true. As John has said at the end of the previous chapter, so much more could have been included in his narrative of Jesus's ministry (20:30). Indeed, in a piece of hyperbole he says the world could not contain the books needed to record all that Jesus did (21:25). However, what John has made unmistakeably clear is that "The Word became flesh and made his dwelling among us. We have seen his glory, the glory of the One and Only, who came from the Father, full of grace and truth" (1:14). And "to all who received him, to those who believed in his name, he gave the right to become children of God" (1:12). That is enough.

Group Discussion Questions

Chapter 1: Overture to the Gospel

The Prologue (John 1:1–18)

1. What do you especially like about the Prologue of John's Gospel?
2. Why do you think John wrote it?
3. What status does it give Jesus?
4. How do you understand Jesus's pre-incarnational life? What meaning do you give to the title *Logos*?
5. What metaphors does John principally use to describe Jesus's ministry?
6. What is the principal role of John the Baptist?
7. How does John describe the people's reactions to the light?
8. What is involved in believing and receiving?
9. What is the glory of the one and only Son?
10. What does receiving grace upon grace mean to you?
11. What does a balanced life of grace and truth look like? What are the pinch points in today's world?

Chapter 2: Great Expectations

John 1:19–51

1. What is the role of John the Baptist and how does he fulfil it? In what ways is John's presentation of the Baptist different from the Synoptic Gospels, and why might that be?
2. What kind of a reaction is there in Israel to John the Baptist?
3. What are the chief qualities of John the Baptist's life and ministry?

4. What two aspects of Jesus's work and ministry does the Baptist highlight? And how are they continued today?
5. How is the new Christian community started and what are the building blocks?
6. What is the merit of "coming and seeing" and how might this work in the Church today?
7. What motivates Andrew and Philip to find and tell Simon Peter and Nathanael?
8. What impresses Nathanael so much? What makes people change their minds about Jesus?

Chapter 3: New Wine in Israel

John 2:1–25

1. Is there any significance to John saying, "on the third day"?
2. Why does Jesus seem at first reluctant to plug the gap in the catering arrangements at the wedding at Cana? What is meant by "my hour has not yet come"?
3. What is the wider significance of the statement, "They have no more wine" (v. 3)? What might it mean metaphorically/spiritually?
4. "Do whatever he tells you." How do we hear Jesus's instructions today?
5. How do you think the miracle occurred?
6. What do we learn from the quantity and quality of the wine created? What part of the Prologue does this event underline?
7. What connection is there between the changing of water into wine and the cleansing of the Temple?
8. What has undermined true Temple worship? What lessons are there in that for the churches today?
9. What is the lesson of the final verses of the chapter (vv. 23–25)?
10. How would you summarize this chapter and its lessons?

Chapter 4: New Birth

John 3:1–36

1. Why is this chapter so prominent in Christian understanding?
2. What is admirable about Nicodemus? How does Jesus treat him?
3. Why is the metaphor of new birth so significant?
4. How does new birth come about? What is the role of the Spirit and Jesus in new birth?
5. Why is the story of the bronze snake so telling in describing the cross?
6. If the verses from John 3:16–21 are John's editorial comment, what do they add to the conversation between Jesus and Nicodemus?
7. In what ways is John the Baptist different from Nicodemus?
8. In several places, John and Jesus distinguish between the earthly and heavenly teaching or testimony (see 3:11–13 and 3:31–33). What does this distinction bring to the Gospel?
9. What do you like best about this chapter?

Chapter 5: The Water of Life

John 4:1–42

1. What is so fresh and attractive about this meeting? What does it teach us about Jesus and how he uses the condition of being human? How does Jesus like to communicate?
2. What do we know about the Samaritans and why they were so despised by the Jews? What was Jesus's attitude to Samaritans? How do we cross boundaries? What examples can we give?
3. Why is water such a good metaphor for salvation? Why are metaphors good ways to communicate? What is Jesus promising?
4. Why does Jesus raise the question of her husband? Why are grace and truth such necessary companions? What does each give to the other?

5. Why is Jesus's description of worship so important? What does worship in spirit and truth look like?
6. What astonishes the disciples on their return? What do the disciples have to learn?
7. Why is the Samaritan woman such an effective evangelist?

Chapter 6: Two Signs and a Discourse

John 4:43–5:47

1. Why do you think that John chose the next two signs as illustrative of Jesus's identity and ministry?
2. What do we especially learn from them?
3. What is striking about this next discourse about Father and Son?
4. People sometimes speak about only doing what they see the Father is doing. This obviously applies to the Son. How might this have worked in practice for Jesus (5:19–20)? And how might this apply to us in practice? Any examples?
5. What do you take away from these verses (5:19–20)?
6. Jesus is described as the life-giver (5:21). What does this mean?
7. "The Father gives judgement to the Son . . . " How does this work and on what basis will judgement be exercised (5:22,28–30)?
8. What is the role of testimony in John's Gospel? Who are the chief givers of testimony as to the Son's identity? What is the chief response that the Gospel is looking for? Why does the Gospel talk about believing rather than faith?
9. What mistake have the Jews made and why (5:39,40,41–46)?
10. How would you summarize this discourse?

Chapter 7: The Bread of Life

John 6:1–71

1. I have described this as the Gospel in a chapter. In what ways might this be true?
2. Why do you think each of the Evangelists include the feeding of the five thousand in their Gospels (6:5–13)?
3. What are the principal lessons from the feeding of the five thousand (6:5–13)?
4. Why do you think many in the crowd respond by trying to make Jesus king? And why is it necessary for Jesus to escape (6:15)?
5. What lessons may be drawn from Jesus walking on the water (6:16–24)?
6. What is the principal lesson that Jesus wants the crowd to learn (6:26–29)?
7. In what ways is Jesus the Bread of Life? What does that mean to you? How are we nourished by this bread (6:35)?
8. What are the implications of the Father giving a disciple to the Son (6:37)?
9. What do we understand by Jesus saying that we must eat of his flesh and drink his blood (6:53–55)? Why was it such an offensive saying to the disciples?
10. How can we account for the different reactions of Simon Peter and Judas Iscariot (6:61–71)? What is the role of the Father, Son and Spirit (6:61–65)?

Chapter 8: Among Divided Opinion: A Universal Offer

John 7:1–52

1. Why did Jesus delay going up to the Feast of Tabernacles?
2. What do you think the feelings in Jerusalem were like at the Feast of Tabernacles?
3. Why were the Jewish authorities so antagonistic to Jesus?

4. In what way was the Feast of Tabernacles an important background to Jesus's great offer of the Spirit?
5. Why is it necessary for Jesus to be glorified (crucified) before the Spirit is universally released?
6. Why does Jesus compare the gift of the Spirit to a stream of living water?
7. How can we live in the midst of this stream and keep it flowing? What can we do to release the flow if it becomes silted?

Chapter 9: Traps, Testimony and True Freedom

John 8:1–59

1. What would you say characterizes this chapter?
2. What is so brilliant in the way Jesus exposes the insincerity of the Jews who bring the woman caught in adultery?
3. How does Jesus deal with her with grace and truth?
4. How is Jesus the Light of the World?
5. What testimony is Jesus looking to in order to corroborate his claims? What is Jesus's relationship with his Father and why is it so critical (8:13–20)?
6. What do the Pharisees not understand about Jesus and at what point will the identity of Jesus be truly revealed (8:27–28)?
7. What makes for true freedom? How could the Jews be children of Abraham and not be free, but worse still, how could they be "of [their] father the devil" (8:44)?
8. How do the Jews or Pharisees respond to Jesus's criticism of them (see 8:48ff.)?
9. What does the claim "before Abraham was born, I am" add to what Jesus says about himself in John's Gospel?
10. What do you take away from this chapter?

Chapter 10: The Man Born Blind

John 9:1–41

1. What was the theological issue that the disciples were struggling with when they saw the man born blind? And how should we approach sickness and disease?
2. Why did John choose this as one of his seven signs? What does it especially illustrate?
3. Why did Jesus choose this method (making a paste for the man's eyes) to heal him? What is implied in the act of washing in the Pool of Siloam?
4. What qualities does the man born blind display in the ensuing controversy? What lies behind the Pharisees' objection? Where has their attitude gone wrong?
5. What do we learn to avoid from this incident? And what do we learn to embrace?
6. How does this sign and controversy fit into the developing narrative of the Gospel?
7. What do you take away from this chapter?

Chapter 11: The Good Shepherd

John 10:1–42

1. Can you discern a train of thought that leads Jesus from John 9 and the healing of the man born blind to the discourse on the Good Shepherd?
2. In what ways does the allegory of the Good Shepherd suit Jesus's purposes?
3. What do his disciples need to understand from the allegory of the Good Shepherd?
4. What are the marks of the Good Shepherd's ministry?

5. What are the differences between the thief and the Good Shepherd? How do we see the effects of their work? What does "fullness of life" look like?
6. What do you expect of a shepherd of God's flock today?
7. What does Jesus say about his relationship with the Father here (vv. 22ff.)? And why does this enrage the Jews?

Chapter 12: The Raising of Lazarus

John 11:1–57

1. Why does Jesus delay before going to his friend Lazarus?
2. What is Jesus's relationship like with the family of Lazarus?
3. How does Jesus manage his relationship as personal friend and Son of God with Lazarus's family?
4. How do Martha and Mary show their different responses to grief? What would you point to? How do they react to Jesus's "late arrival"?
5. What is the great truth of which this is a sign? How do we understand it?
6. Why does Jesus weep?
7. What strikes you about the raising of Lazarus? What is the difference between the raising of this dead man and the resurrection?
8. What are the varied responses to this astounding miracle?

Chapter 13: The Turning Point

John 12:1–50

1. What aspects of this chapter indicate that it is a chapter of transition?
2. How do you understand the anointing of Jesus by Mary?
3. What contrasts can you draw between Judas Iscariot and Mary?

4. What has found its way into the hearts of the Chief Priests? Why is this?
5. What is the significance of Jesus's entry into Jerusalem?
6. Why is the time for interviews with some Greeks over?
7. What hour has come?
8. How will the Father be glorified in the death of Jesus and how will Jesus glorify the Father?
9. Why do people not believe?
10. How does Jesus summarize his teaching?

Chapter 14: A New Way and a New Commandment

John 13:1–38

1. How does John introduce the washing of the disciples' feet (vv. 1–4)?
2. Why does John concentrate on the washing of the disciples' feet, rather than on the institution of the Last Supper?
3. What does the example of Jesus teach us?
4. How might this translate into everyday action?
5. Why does Jesus reveal Judas's anticipated betrayal?
6. In what ways is the New Commandment different from the Great Commandment?
7. Why has the Church found it so difficult to obey the New Commandment?
8. What lies at the root of Peter's forthcoming failure?
9. How would you summarize the teaching of this chapter?

Chapter 15: The Trinity Revealed

John 14:1–31

1. What are the sentiments behind this chapter?
2. What does Jesus have to clarify for Thomas?
3. What do the disciples, and in particular Philip, have to understand about the relationship between the Father and the Son?
4. What helps you to understand the unity of the Father and Son? In what respects are there no differences between the Father and the Son? In what respects are there differences?
5. What does the Father give the Son (words and actions, see verses 10 and 11)? What does that mean?
6. In what ways will the Church do "greater things"?
7. What is the relationship of love and obedience?
8. What will the function of the Spirit be? How do we experience him?
9. What are the advantages of Jesus going away? What must the disciples experience in the meantime?
10. How would you summarize this chapter?

Chapter 16: The True Vine

John 15:1–27

1. Why is the allegory of the vine such a good one for describing the dynamics of discipleship?
2. What does "abiding" or "remaining" in the vine amount to? Can you give any practical examples?
3. What does "pruning" mean in practice and how might we have experienced it? Can anyone give a description from their own lives?
4. What form does the fruit take? What is its effect? What warnings are there in this allegory?

5. What is the relationship between love and obedience from verse 9ff.? The result of knowing God's love is joy (see verse 11). How is that experienced?
6. What is the difference between servants and friends? How do we understand the friendship of God?
7. How does Jesus now prepare his disciples for the future (verse 18ff.)? What can they expect? What comfort can they expect if facing trouble?
8. What are your overall impressions from this chapter? How might it help in our discipleship today?

Chapter 17: Assistance at Hand: Joy Awaits

John 16:1–33

1. As you look back on your life, what have been your notable leavings and new beginnings, and how did they affect you?
2. Although the disciples will face grief of various kinds, it will be to their advantage that Jesus goes away. How are both these things fulfilled? Why are departures a necessary, if difficult, part of life?
3. What are the activities of the Advocate and how do you see them working?
4. How does this process of convincing and convicting work (see 16:8–11)?
5. How do Father, Son and Spirit work together (see 16:12–15)?
6. How is the analogy of a woman giving birth an apt one for the forthcoming experience of the disciples? How can grief turn to joy in our own lives?
7. What distinction does Jesus draw between figurative teaching and plain teaching? Why might one be more appropriate at certain times?
8. How is Jesus encouraging his disciples to think differently about prayer (16:26,27)?
9. In what terms does Jesus see his mission here, and how does this tie in with what has gone before in this Gospel (16:28)?

10. Do the disciples really have an epiphany moment or are they simply keen to show that they have understood? Have we had moments of great spiritual clarity when our understanding has fallen into place (16:29–32)?
11. What final encouragement does Jesus leave the disciples with at the very end of his Upper Room and Temple discourse? What notes does Jesus strike (16:33)?

Chapter 18: Jesus's Prayer for the Church

John 17:1–26

1. How do you imagine this prayer taking place? What role does it have in the preparation of the disciples?
2. How would you describe eternal life from these words of Jesus, and what does that mean for you (see verse 3)?
3. Four times in these opening verses Jesus speaks of "glory". How do you understand this idea of glory?
4. The key words in the second part of the prayer (verses 6–10) are "give", "know" and "words". What do these words and their use by Jesus convey to you?
5. What kind of protection (verses 11–18) is Jesus praying for? What blessings and challenges can the disciples expect?
6. What does being "sanctified in the truth" mean?
7. What are Jesus's prayers and hopes for the future of the Church? Why is "complete unity" so difficult to achieve and what might it mean?
8. What is Jesus's long-term ambition for the Church?
9. What does making Jesus known involve?
10. What is your overall "take-away" from this prayer?

Chapter 19: Arrest, Trials, and Peter's Denial

John 18:1–19:16

1. What strikes you about John's account of the arrest of Jesus?
2. Compare the reaction of Jesus to the response of his disciples and the intention of the detachment from the Jewish hierarchy.
3. Why is Peter so vulnerable? In what ways can we deny Jesus in our own lives?
4. What is the focus of the trial before Annas?
5. Why is Pilate such a reluctant judge of Jesus?
6. What are the main issues in the trial of Jesus before Pilate?
7. What prevents Pilate from releasing Jesus?
8. What do you take away from observing the conduct of Jesus in these trials?

Chapter 20: The Crucifixion

John 19:16b–42

1. What aspects of the crucifixion does John especially draw out?
2. What do the words from the cross in John's account tell us about the spiritual reality of the crucifixion?
3. What do Pilate, the soldiers and the family of Jesus contribute to the inner meaning of the crucifixion?
4. What is "finished"?
5. What is John at pains to describe about the actual death of Jesus?
6. How far has Nicodemus come in his journey of faith since his conversation with Jesus in Chapter 3?
7. What can we learn from Jewish burial customs?
8. How best can we think about the meaning of the crucifixion?

Chapter 21: The Day of Resurrection

John 20:1–31

1. What is John at pains to record about the empty tomb and why?
2. How are the differences between John and Peter revealed in this description?
3. What do you understand by the resurrection?
4. What is the significance of Mary Magdalene being the first witness?
5. In Jesus's first appearance to the disciples, he moves them on in their mission: in what ways does he do this?
6. How does the Church make known and offer forgiveness of sins today?
7. What kind of character is Thomas? And what kind of doubt does he display?
8. How do you think Thomas feels during his encounter with Jesus the following week?
9. How does John end the main part of his Gospel?

Chapter 22: The Epilogue: The World Awaits

John 21:1–25

1. Why do you think John chooses these two episodes (the catch of fish and the restoration of Peter) to end his Gospel? What is the point of an epilogue?
2. What does the great catch of fish signify and what lessons does the story illustrate?
3. Why is the restoration of Peter so important? Why do you think the Gospel ends with it?
4. How much should we read into the different Greek words for love in the account (i.e., Jesus using mostly *agapaō* and Peter using *philéo* in reply)?
5. Why is love the root of all discipleship?

6. What does "feeding my sheep" (or lambs) involve?
7. Why do we never graduate from being "followers"?
8. What have you enjoyed most or learnt especially from studying St John's Gospel?
9. What has changed for you?

In the same series:

ISBN: 9781789590449

GOSPEL *of*
FULFILMENT
Exploring the Gospel of
Matthew

Patrick Whitworth

ISBN: 9781789591798

GOSPEL *of the*
KINGDOM
Exploring the Gospel of
Mark

Patrick Whitworth

GOSPEL *for the*
OUTSIDER
The Gospel in
Luke & Acts

Patrick Whitworth

ISBN: 9781908381248

GOSPEL *of the*
TRINITY
Exploring the Gospel of
John

Patrick Whitworth

ISBN: 9781789592825

www.sacristy.co.uk

Sacristy
Press

EU GPSR Authorized Representative:

LOGOS EUROPE, 9 rue Nicolas Poussin, 17000 La Rochelle, France

contact@logoseurope.eu

www.ingramcontent.com/pod-product-compliance
Lightning Source LLC
Chambersburg PA
CBHW070330090426
42733CB00012B/2421